WINSTON CUP

1994

ACKNOWLEDGMENTS

Dear Race Fans,

The 1994 NASCAR Winston Cup season will always hold a special place in the hearts of race fans worldwide. Dale Earnhardt equaled a mark that was thought to be unattainable; he tied "King" Richard Petty's record of seven championships. For the first time the NASCAR drivers held a race at The Brickyard, Indianapolis Motor Speedway. Fans everywhere were saddened with the loss of Neil Bonnett and Rodney Orr.

Every year countless people work behind the scenes and long hours every weekend to bring you the most exciting motorsports in the world. We would like to take a minute to thank them.

First of all our thanks go out Mr. Bill France, Mr. Jim France, Mr. Brian France, Mr. Les Richter, Mr. Bill Seaborn, and Mr. Paul Schaefer. Their help and support are greatly appreciated.

Secondly, thanks to all the folks at the R.J. Reynolds Tobacco Co. including Mr. T. Wayne Robertson, Jeff Byrd, Greg Littell, John Powell, Larry Prillaman, Steve Tucker, Curtis Gray, Chris Powell, Dennis Dawson and Randy Chapel. These people travel countless miles each year for you.

Once again Mr. Bob Kelly wrote this book. Bob's dedication is unmatched and we thank him for his efforts. The beautiful photography in this book is the combined effort of several photographers. They race almost as fast as the drivers to get just the right shot. Mr. Kenny Kane, Mr. Ernie Masche, and Mr. David Chobat, we thank you.

Finally, and mostly importantly we thank YOU! The NASCAR Winston Cup fans. Without your support and input this book would not be possible.

This book is for you, Please enjoy.

Winston Cup '94 Staff: Ivan Mothershead, Publisher; Charlie Keiger, Associate Publisher; Bob Kelly, Senior Editor; Amy Vail, Senior Editor, Production manager; Jeff Huneycutt, Ward Woodbury, Associate Editors; Brett Shippy, Mike McBride, Paul Bond, Layout - Design; Mark Cantey, Henry Boardman, Mary Cartee, Mary Alice Costner, Shelley McDaniel, Lewis Patton.

FOREWORD

BILL FRANCE

"**THE INAUGURAL NASCAR WINSTON CUP SERIES BRICKYARD 400 AT INDIANAPOLIS MOTOR SPEEDWAY WAS A SIGNIFICANT MOMENT IN THE HISTORY OF MOTORSPORTS WORLDWIDE.**"

• • • • • • • • • • • • • • • •

A new era dawned for the NASCAR Winston Cup Series in 1994.

Certainly, this season will be remembered for Dale Earnhardt's record-tying seventh NASCAR Winston Cup Series championship. But 1994 also will be remembered as the year NASCAR racing boldly marched into the future.

The inaugural NASCAR Winston Cup Series Brickyard 400 at Indianapolis Motor Speedway was a significant moment in the history of motorsports worldwide. Jeff Gordon's win in the celebrated event underscores the bright new era we have entered.

The NASCAR Winston Cup Series produced three first-time winners in 1994: Sterling Marlin in the season-opening Daytona 500; Jeff Gordon in the Coca-Cola 600 at Charlotte; and Jimmy Spencer in the DieHard 500 at Talladega.

First-year owner/drivers enjoyed success as Geoff Bodine and Ricky Rudd each won races. In addition, past NASCAR Winston Cup champions Terry Labonte and Bill Elliott returned to victory lane. In all, a dozen different drivers shared NASCAR Winston Cup Series victory lanes in 1994, and 17 drivers won Busch Pole Awards.

NASCAR and our marketing partners reached out to new NASCAR fans like never before this year, expanding an enthusiastic fan base already known to be the most loyal in major league sports. This would not have been possible without the commitment to excellence from our NASCAR Winston Cup Series track operators, team owners, drivers, crews and their sponsors.

We are proud that through teamwork, we made the 1994 NASCAR Winston Cup season the dawn of the next great era in NASCAR racing. The pages that follow chronicle an unfolding story that is certain to continue in 1995.

Sincerely,
Bill France

N A S C A R

Table of Contents

Hardee's returned to NASCAR Winston Cup racing— backing Rookie Of The Year contender Ward Burton.

While Dale Earnhardt reaped the rewards of his sixth NASCAR Winston Cup championship, the Richard Childress team prepared for its quest of a third consecutive title. So many changes were made within other teams that it appeared fans would need a program to keep it all straight.

In all, more than 30 teams had undergone changes in drivers, cars, crew chiefs or motor programs — even the garage area at The Beach had a decidedly different appearance.

Here's a quick look at the major changes that would have a bearing on the season-opener:

1 — Skoal renewed with Richard Jackson's team for an additional three years, and Rick Mast would begin the season with a new crew chief, Kevin Hamlin.

2 — Rusty Wallace, after winning 10 races for Pontiac, switched his Roger Penske-owned team to Ford. Although the team remained intact, the big question was how quickly Rusty could get back to the winner's circle after the change of manufacturers.

3 — Sterling Marlin replaced the Jeff Purvis/Joe Nemechek/Jimmy Hensley triumvirate that had finished the '93 season in the Morgan-McClure Kodak Chevrolets following Ernie Irvan's departure. The reunion of old friends is expected to give Sterling his first career NASCAR Winston Cup victory in 1994.

4 — Terry Labonte took over the Hendrick Motorsports ride from Ricky Rudd, and Kellogg's replaced Tide as the primary sponsor.

5 — Geoff Bodine, preparing for his first full season in a dual role as both car owner and driver, found sponsorship from both Exide Batteries and Montgomery Ward. In 1994, Bodine also would be the leading flag-waver for Hoosier tires when the company returned to NASCAR Winston Cup competition.

6 — After his move up from the NASCAR Busch Series Grand National Division ranks, Jeff Burton replaced Sterling Marlin at Stavola Brothers Racing. Burton was just one of several drivers who would make the jump from triple-A to the majors.

7 — Ricky Rudd took over the former Bob Whitcomb Racing number and would drive Fords in the Tide colors. He watched as his new team began to take shape in rented quarters while his own shop was being built. Rudd was hopeful that new crew chief Bill Ingle, who left Bahari Racing in August 1992, would be able to put the right people together to give the Virginian a chance to win in his first season as car owner and driver. Ingle had not worn the crew chief's hat in more than a year.

8 — After losing Meineke to the Hedrick team and '93 driver Jimmy Spencer to Junior Johnson, Bobby Allison Motorsports regrouped for 1994. Bobby named Chuck Bown as his driver, and the team headed to Daytona still searching for a sponsor for their black Fords.

9 — John Andretti would compete for the full season in Billy Hagan's Chevrolets, but sponsorship was scarce. After Pete Wright left the team to work for the new Travis Carter team, Hagan hired Ingle as the crew chief for Andretti. Then Ingle pulled up stakes to head Rudd's crew. So when the team headed for Daytona, Doug Williams, from Junie Donlavey's shop in Richmond, had been named the new crew chief.

10 — Bud Moore's Thunderbirds had a new look for '94 after the blue Ford Quality Care colors replaced the familiar red of Motorcraft Parts and Service. Lake Speed, who had replaced the departed Geoff Bodine in the last few races of '93, would be behind the wheel for the full season.

11 — Ted Musgrave, replacing Wally Dallenbach Jr., was named the new driver for Jack Roush's other team. And new Family Channel colors would be painted on the car, replacing Keystone beer's sponsorship.

12 — Loy Allen Jr., who raced a few '93 events in Naturally Fresh colors, readied for his rookie season with

Hooters, which was returning with its familiar orange, white and brown colors. Allen's team merged with Tri-Star and, along with Hoosier tires, was expected to challenge at many tracks in 1994.

13 — Bobby Labonte and Bill Davis retained the Maxwell House colors, but nearly everything else had changed. The team changed from Ford to Pontiac sheetmetal during the off-season and Chris Hussey replaced Tim Brewer as crew chief.

14 — Travis Carter formed his own team, bringing the purple and yellow colors of Camel and Smokin' Joe's to the circuit. Pete Wright moved from Hagan Racing to become the chief wrench for Travis, and Hut Stricklin was named the driver during a November press conference at Phoenix.

15 — Junior Johnson, trying to put some teeth in the "Big Mac Attack", got the aggressive driver he was looking for when he lured Jimmy Spencer away from the Bobby Allison Motorsports team. Junior expected Spencer to put the McDonald's Ford in the winner's circle on a regular basis in '94.

16 — After a nine-race "test session" at the conclusion of 1993, all systems were "go" for Ernie Irvan, who would be behind the controls of Robert Yates' Havoline Ford. The group had worked well together during the final third of the '93 season, and the team was rated one of the favorites for the championship in preseason media polls.

17 — Another new team for 1994 was the Diamond Ridge effort. Construction magnate Gary Bechtel enlisted the help of crew chief Marc Reno to prepare Chevrolets for Busch Grand National Champion Steve Grissom. Despite the rookie status of the team, many expected the effort to be a strong one from the start.

18 — Hardee's restaurants returned to NASCAR Winston Cup to back Ward Burton and his team, who were newly graduated from the NASCAR Busch Series. Tom Fox, who had headed the Hoosier research and development program during 1993, was named as the crew chief for the A.G. Dillard-owned team.

19 — The Active Trucking team enlisted the services of stalwart Dick Trickle after giving Jimmy Horton the boot, but the team began the season with no sponsorship. Could Trickle, with his immense experience, lead the team to victory lane?

20 — Harry Gant entered his "farewell" season determined to improve his record. Harry's final year would be only the team's second season of fielding Chevrolets (after switching from Oldsmobiles), and Gant could only hope he would be able to reward his legions of fans with a final trip to the winner's circle.

21 — Kenny Wallace and Dirt Devil had departed, so owner Felix Sabates took Bobby Hamilton to Daytona, hoping to find sponsorship for his Pontiac team. It would be a second chance at NASCAR Winston Cup racing for

Hamilton.

22 — After leaving Bobby Allison Motorsports, Meineke Mufflers landed at Larry and Sue Hedrick's team. Together, they were able to sign Joe Nemechek. With Waddell Wilson building the power and Doug Richert the crew chief, the team had all the makings of a winner. All it would take was time for the group to come together.

23 — NASCAR approved a new rear deck for the Pontiacs, and Kyle Petty, the only Poncho driver to win in 1993 (other than Rusty's 10 wins) was expected to be the standard-bearer for the Tin Indian Troupe. Mello Yello had signed an extension of its contracts, and now it was up to Kyle and the team to produce.

24 — Back to the familiar car number after running "44" for a season, Richard Petty hoped his team's fortunes would change for the better. He had replaced driver Rick Wilson with Wally Dallenbach Jr. and promised better results from the team in 1994.

25 — Phoenix Racing would provide the Chevrolets for Neil Bonnett, who was returning to competition in a few selected races. Country Time Lemonade agreed to sponsor the car, and the team would be crewed during race weekends by Dale Earnhardt's NASCAR Busch Series crew.

26 — When D.K. Ulrich decided to form a second team, he took Jasper and USAir with him. Ray and Dane DeWitt signed Jimmy Hensley to lead the No. 55 team for the season and headed to Daytona looking for sponsorship.

27 — Butch Mock bought out his longtime partner Bob Rahilly and began construction on a new race shop. Todd Bodine would begin his first full season behind the wheel of the Factory Stores of America Ford, and Mock hired Troy Selburg as the team's crew chief.

28 — D. K. Ulrich's new team carried a different number, and Greg Sacks signed on as the driver for the USAir and Jasper Engines-sponsored Ford team. The group had been extremely fast during test sessions at Daytona and would begin the season on Hoosier tires.

29 — After a year of struggling, it now appeared that Cale Yarborough's team was off on the right foot. Fingerhut had signed on as the team's sponsor for the next three years, and Cale hired Ken Glenn as the team's new crew chief. Derrike Cope would finally have good engines and equipment to help him return to the form he displayed in 1990 when he won the Daytona 500 and Dover races.

After an off-season that included the most wholesale changes in drivers and teams in recent memory, one had to excuse team members and crew chiefs — not to mention drivers — when they headed, out of habit, for the wrong transporters and cars in the Daytona garage! It would take more than a few minutes for everyone to acclimate themselves to their new roles in 1994!

Remembering

NEIL BONNETT
& RODNEY ORR

NEIL BONNETT

1946 - 1994

The losses of Neil Bonnett and Rodney Orr still weigh heavily on the hearts of all whom they had touched.

Fans who hadn't followed the sport before 1990 knew Neil only as a face and a voice brought into the family room by television. As the host of The Nashville Network's "Winners," a weekly half-hour show, Neil crossed every motorsports line, giving viewers the chance to learn more about every type of motorsport and meet the varied competitors. Following his accident at Darlington in 1990, Neil became the foundation of "Winners," and he brought his natural humility and compassion with him when he filmed the shows. He had enormous respect for racing and the people involved with it, and in every interview, it was obvious that the respect was mutual.

From 1990-94, Neil worked hard to become one of the best analysts the sport has ever known. He constantly made self-deprecating jokes about his work behind the microphone, but his growth, maturity and self-confidence in front of the camera came as quickly and naturally as his success in the

A season expected to feature unparalleled competition for the NASCAR Winston Cup championship had barely begun when the sport lost two members of its racing family: one was among the sport's most visible heroes; the other was a young talent expected to play an important part in the future of stock car racing.

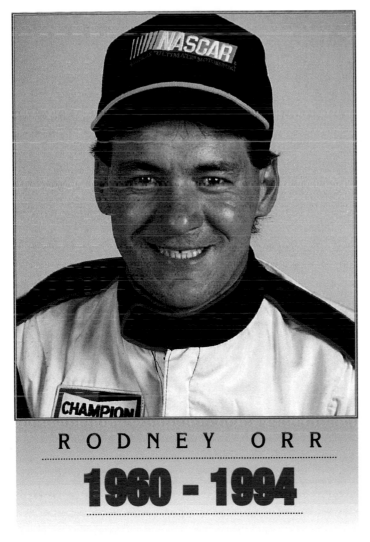

R O D N E Y   O R R
1960 - 1994

ate and engaging that he became friends with everyone who crossed his path. He never forgot a name and always had a smile and a handshake or a hug for an acquaintance. After an episode of "Winners" late last year, when he signed off as "Cecil B. DeBonnett," complete with ascot, beret and fake French accent, a writer teased him at Phoenix. He grinned that Bonnett grin and said, "Yeah, can you imagine how many French viewers we lost after they heard me?"

Despite his success off the track, his passion for racing never diminished, and it led him back to the driver's seat at Daytona in February. Neil's credo for life was to do the very best he could every day of his life, whether that be as a television commentator, a race driver, a businessman, a father and husband or a hunting and fishing companion. For everyone who knew him through the years, there is no doubt that he personified that philosophy.

The sense of loss expressed in Hueytown and Bessemer, AL, sadly was echoed a few days later in tiny Robbinsville, NC, a town of 751 residents nestled in the Great Smoky Mountains between Asheville, NC, and Knoxville, TN. Rodney Orr had not yet made his NASCAR Winston Cup debut, but he already had won a NASCAR championship.

After winning more than 300 events in motocross features, Orr turned to four wheels, competing regularly at Volusia County Speedway after he and his father moved their heavy equipment business to Palm Coast, FL, just north of Daytona.

Rodney's NASCAR outings began in 1991 in the NASCAR Goody's Dash Series, where he made six starts. He upgraded his program in 1992, running 14 races and finishing in the top five two times. He also won the Goody's Dash Series Most Popular Driver award. In 1993, he blitzed his way to the series championship, winning twice and posting 11 top five finishes in 16 starts in his Pontiac.

He had planned to move into the NASCAR Busch Grand National Series in 1994, but since V-6 engines were being phased out prior to the 1995 season, he decided that, rather than invest in equipment that would quickly become outmoded, he would purchase a NASCAR Winston Cup car and run selected events, beginning with the Daytona 500.

During preseason testing, Rodney felt he had the right combination: his Ford and engines from Ernie Elliott. He turned the seventh-fastest time in testing prior to Daytona.

Like Neil, Rodney was a man of simple desires. He took pride in his small-town roots and was a man who never forgot the friends who helped him along the way. For their friends, families and fans, the losses of Rodney, whose star was on the rise, and Neil, who had been known and loved throughout his 20-year NASCAR Winston Cup career, will not be easily overcome.

early '80s as a NASCAR Winston Cup driver.

When CBS and TNN offered him work as an analyst and host for "Winners," Neil knew that he might never get back into a race car. But he attacked his new tasks with the same ferocity and unassuming humility with which he had forged his driving career. Despite the fact that Neil was one of the most determined and competitive drivers to ever belt into a race car, millions of fans may remember him best for his ability to describe what happened on the track with words and phrases that were clearly understood in living rooms across the country.

Neil would never want to be remembered for anything other than his ability to drive the wheels off a race car, but for millions, his legacy will be his television talent.

He was also one of the very best behind the wheel, and few who saw him in the Wood Brothers Mercurys and Fords, the Rahmoc Chevrolets and Pontiacs or Junior Johnson's Chevrolets will ever forget the tenacity that took Neil to victory lane after victory lane around the NASCAR Winston Cup tour.

Neil was part of the NASCAR Winston Cup family for more than two decades, and his nature was so compassion-

ere we are, weeks after we were able to clinch the 1994 NASCAR Winston Cup Championship at Rockingham, and I'm still amazed.

Unless you've competed on the NASCAR Winston Cup level, you can't imagine how difficult it is to win a championship. While growing up and even while racing at this level — winning races and titles — Richard Petty's record of seven championships looked unapproachable. That feat, as well as his record of 200 wins, were marks everyone thought would never been equaled or surpassed.

But, one step at a time, we've been able to win titles; with each one, we edged closer to The King's record of seven. This year, thanks to the consistency of the Richard Childress team, we were able to win a seventh title and tie Richard's mark.

That's what I'm amazed by. I'm not much different than anyone else. When I started racing, it wasn't to try to tie Richard Petty's number of titles. I started because it was

in my blood and because I had grown up around it. I didn't like school. I wanted to be working on my dad's race car. I wanted to go racing myself.

Just like tens of thousands of others who race every week at short tracks around the country, I started with what I could scrape together. I borrowed money to race, and if I didn't win enough to pay it back the following week, I owed people until I could pay them. I learned on dirt, moved up to asphalt and kept following my dream. Little by little, step by step, I kept moving upwards. Looking back, it seems like such an unbelievable journey. I think about it often. I am so fortunate to be doing what I do and to be successful. Hundreds of thousands of other racers will never make it, mostly through no fault of their own. It's just like any other sport. The right break has to come at the right time, and enough people have to believe in you to help make it happen for you.

This journey has been so much more than it started out to be. Then, I was just a hobby racer, trying to win on the dirt and asphalt tracks on weekends near my hometown of Kannapolis. It is hard for me to believe that now, since Richard Childress and I got together, we have won six NASCAR Winston Cups during the last nine years. I truly am amazed.

This was a season of unbelievable highs and lows. Winning the NASCAR Winston Cup took us to the highest level imaginable, particularly winning it as early in the season as we did.

But losing my best friend, Neil Bonnett, right at the beginning of the season also made this year one of the most difficult I've ever been through. Last year, when we lost Davey Allison and Alan Kulwicki, all of us in the sport suffered a lot. But with Neil being gone, this year was even harder for me, my team and my family, not to mention Neil's family.

For more than a year, Neil had been a behind-the-scenes part of the Childress team and had done an enormous amount of testing and development for us. So our team suffered a huge blow in February from a professional standpoint as well.

For Neil's family, for my own, for Richard Childress' and the Allisons, it was something that, to this day,

1994
NASCAR
Winston Cup
Goodwrench
1994
Winston Cup Champions
Winston
Cup Series
NASCAR
1994
NASCAR
Winston Cup
Champion
1994
Winston Cup Champion
Dale Earnhardt
1994
NASCAR
Winston Cup

The Holly Farms 400 at North Wilkesboro was the fifth in a string of races that proved critical to Wallace's bid for the championship. During that series, Wallace posted three wins, a fourth and a seventh but gained only five points on Dale Earnhardt.

here to share in the championship week in New York with us. But I know he'll be with us in spirit and will always be with me and our team.

Right from the get-go this season, it was clear that we were going to have to fight not only Rusty Wallace for the championship (again!), but that Ernie Irvan was going to be a major factor with the Robert Yates team. It didn't take a rocket scientist to see that Ernie and the Yates bunch fit well together in the final third of last year, so we expected them to be strong contenders this season. And we expected Mark Martin to be a factor in the championship. Mark and that entire Jack Roush team are too good not to contend.

There were some others that we didn't know about: Kyle Petty, Bill Elliott, Jimmy Spencer and Kenny Schrader. You couldn't count Terry Labonte out of the hunt, especially after his career got a new breath of life with a good team like the Hendrick bunch. And Jeff Gordon and his team had the makings, too.

Then there was the Goodyear/Hoosier situation. It became evident at Daytona that the Hoosiers were going to be mighty fast, and who knew what would happen as the season progressed?

We didn't win the Daytona 500 — again! — but we ran well, and only a handling problem late in the race kept us from a run at Sterling Marlin. By the time we finished at Atlanta, we were third in the points. Some little problems had kept us from winning: a slight brake problem and loose lug nuts at Rockingham, off just a little at Richmond and a jack-screw that backed out at Atlanta and caused handling problems.

But we got it going at Darlington. We won the 400-miler — our first victory since the second Talladega race last season. We moved into second place then; the crew had made some great decisions about the chassis and controlling tire wear. At Bristol, we came back with another victory — the first time we had won on a short track since 1991. It was a great win because it came with a car we'd never raced before. That victory was my eighth career win at Bristol.

At North Wilkesboro, we fought back from being nearly lapped to battle with Ricky Rudd at the end. At Martinsville, we spun and had the overflow gas can stuck on the back of the car, which brought us in for a stop and cost us a lap. We fell to second, 25 behind Ernie.

remains an unbelievable loss. It will always be that way for us. Nothing makes it better.

During the last several years, Neil and I became extremely close friends. We hunted and fished together on a regular basis. I know that the time I took away from my family and business interests to spend with Neil were stolen moments. But my wife, Teresa, and my family understood that those hours and days were of great importance to me. Some days, just Neil and I would hunt or fish together; other times, we would invite a few close friends. Either way, those treasured occasions provided a relaxing escape from the pressures of the racing world. I will never be able to thank Teresa enough for understanding. And under the circumstances, I realize I was blessed to have spent the time with him that I did. Looking back now, I would hate it if we had not been able to share the time and friendship that we did.

In the past, I've dedicated championships to my dad, to my mom, to my family, to the fans, to the crew members. This one, because of what has happened and the contribution Neil made to our entire team with his research and development testing over the previous year, is dedicated to my friend Neil Bonnett. I only wish he was

At Talladega, we came in for tires, started 11th with 21 laps to go and went right to the front. We made the right moves when we needed to and out-ran Michael Waltrip, Ernie and Spencer to get our third win of the year. It was one of the most exciting races I've ever been in, and it gave us a chance to win the Winston Select Million — if we could win at Charlotte and Darlington.

At Sears Point, we came home third, a really solid showing. Then we wrecked with Rusty in the Winston Select. Fortunately for both of us, the race didn't pay points! At Charlotte, I bumped Mark as he slowed to pit, causing some nose damage and starting a nine car fracas. We finished ninth.

Then came Dover, and we took a licking on the one-mile track. I wrecked when I cut a right-front tire, and despite the team's repairs, we finished 75 laps behind in 28th place. We lost more than 100 points there. When we left, we were 163 behind.

It was time to take off the gloves. We finished second at Pocono, second at Michigan, third at Daytona and second at New Hampshire. When we left the Bahre's track in New England, we were back in the point lead. We got a little help from Ernie's incident, but we had to really fight to get that finish. The car didn't handle well, and it was overheating. Ernie lapped us, but one lap later, he got tangled up with Ward Burton. That put us in the lead lap. I had been in an early tangle with Derrike Cope, but we came back to lead the race twice for 30 laps and then just barely lose to Rudd at the end.

At Pocono, the second time, we finished seventh and built our point lead to 93 over Ernie. We got our second pole of the year at Talladega, but after just 80 laps, our engine failed for the first time. Ernie returned to the point lead, and we were 16 behind when we went to Indianapolis.

The Brickyard 400 was one of the races we most wanted to win during the season, but I scraped the wall on the fourth turn and spent the rest of the race fighting my way back through the field. We stripped a lug nut on another stop, so I had to fight through the field again. In all, the crew did a great job, and we were able to finish fifth and take the point lead again.

At The Glen we finished third with a little help from the late-race fracas between Rusty and Wally Dallenbach. We led early there, but we weren't any different from anyone else at the end of the race. Nobody had anything for Mark that day.

Then at Michigan, the entire complexion of the season changed. We were leading Ernie by 27 going into Michigan, but after his accident, we were suddenly way ahead of Mark and Rusty. During the race itself, we were involved in an accident with Todd Bodine and completed only about a quarter of the race to finish 37th.

Fortunately, Ernie is making an incredible recovery. But

The 1994 championship is the sixth for Richard Childress and the Goodwrench team. Dale credits much of his success to the team's hard work and preparation: They provided him with reliable, consistent cars throughout the season.

Dale Earnhardt scored a pair of third-place finishes on the road courses: first, here at Sears Point and then at Watkins Glen.

the battle for the NASCAR Winston Cup had changed. After Michigan, Mark was 206 behind and Rusty 213 behind, and we were in the driver's seat. We knew we were going to race those two in every event for the rest of the season, but if we could maintain the quality of preparation and the consistency of the cars, we could be on the way to the championship. It was another turning point for the team. If we had good luck, we would be in the title hunt to the end. But if we had bad luck, the others could still easily catch us.

The stretch run to the title was upon us, and the Childress team was determined to win the title. At Bristol, we were third; at Darlington, we missed the Winston $100,000 bonus when we finished second after Bill Elliott ran us down at the end. At Richmond, we were third again, beating Rusty on the last two laps. At Dover, we finished second under caution, almost out of gas, to Rusty, who had a flat tire and was nearly out of gas, too! Another lap and maybe neither of us would have finished!

Martinsville saw a great race with Rusty during the final 25 laps. I was determined to win — and so was he! It was great stuff, and we got another second place. We spun twice but still had a great day. At North Wilkesboro, I collided with Jeff Burton on a restart — my fault — and we finished seventh.

Going to Charlotte, we had 208 points on Rusty. Mark had suffered some bad luck and was now 423 behind. The Goodwrench team had really come through in the stretch run. Then Rusty lost an engine at Charlotte, and we finished third despite crunching the front end of the car (I hit Elliott in a melee on the track). We tried to win that race — and we did pick up three positions in the final four laps — but we ran out of time.

Headed for Rockingham, we were 321 ahead; for the first time since 1987, we were in a position to clinch the title before the end of the season — if everything went right. Rusty had another engine problem, and when the race was over, I had led four times for 108 laps but had to fight off Rick Mast in the closing laps to win for the first time since the Talladega race in May.

It was a special win for us because it was the first time I had won the fall race at Rockingham, and I was happy to win at Frank Wilson's track. Frank, the president of Rockingham, had died earlier in the season, and he had been a good friend of mine. He had been helpful to me throughout my career. Winning Frank's race made it special for me.

During the final third of the season, we didn't qualify nearly as well as we wanted. A lot of reporters wanted to know if I was concerned about that part of the race, especially because we were leading in the point race. I was to some degree; when you're in the second half of the field, you have extra worries about getting in someone else's mess. But we were the defending champs, we always had first choice of the pits, and I knew that it wouldn't take very long for my "over-the-wall" gang to get me toward the front when it came time for pit stops. That, and the fact that I had good race cars, was enough to make me secure in the belief that I would be able to make up for the qualifying positions.

The guys on the crew really worked hard all year to give me good machinery and keep the cars consistent throughout the year. That's one thing that Richard Childress and this team do so well. Consistency is the key to the titles, and if you want to win a championship, you have to finish well in each race. Every race is important, and you have to take each one as it comes and get the best finish you can from it. Richard and the Goodwrench team have learned how to win championships.

Everyone knows that Richard and I have a unique relationship. We may be car owner and driver, but we are also extremely close friends. There's nothing that I wouldn't do for Richard, nor him for me. I guess that's why winning races and championships is so special to me. When Richard raced, he never won either a championship or a race. He was a talented driver but never had the right combination to win. Now, every victory and every championship is something that is really special for me to be a part of with him.

Much of the reason for our success is the work of the crew and the preparation of the cars. Some of it was good racing luck on the track. But mostly, it was the work in the shop and at the track by the Goodwrench team.

Now, for the third time, we all have the opportunity to try to win three consecutive NASCAR Winston Cup titles. The only other person who has done that is Cale Yarborough, and all of us would like to tie that record. If we did, it would be the seventh championship for this team and the eighth for me. Now wouldn't that be something to be amazed about!

One of the best things that happened during the season for Richard, for myself and for the team was the support from you, the race fan. At the beginning of the season, your support was really important as the team rallied from losing Neil. In the middle of the summer, when we were so far behind after Dover, your support helped us get going again. And during the stretch run, you helped us maintain the level of intensity needed to run well every week and get to the position of winning the title.

But more than for just ourselves and our team, all of us also want to thank you for the outpouring of cards, letters, telephone calls and support for Susan Bonnett and her family, and for Ernie and his family. You'll never understand just how important that support was to helping Susan and Ernie and their families make it through such tough times. Race fans simply are unbelievable, and we'd like to take this time to thank you for helping when help was needed most.

Dale Earnhardt
1994 Winston Cup Champion

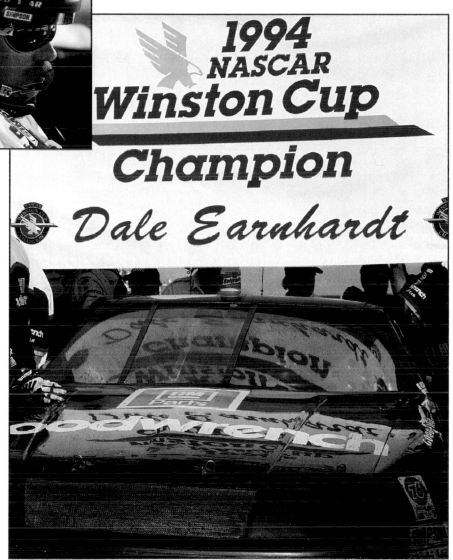

DAYTONA 500

DAYTONA
INTERNATIONAL SPEEDWAY

FEBRUARY 20, 1994

No one knew just what to expect when the teams unloaded their transporters at Daytona for the beginning of Speedweeks. Not only had there been enormous personnel and sponsor turnover within the teams, but yet another variable had been added to the mix:

Hoosier had returned to NASCAR Winston Cup racing.

The Indiana-based tire company had collaborated with a development team during the 1993 season, and owner Bob Newton insisted his tires would be competitive, if not superior to Goodyears, from the first race.

Well, it was time to find out.

(Above) In front of a packed house, Dale Jarrett (18) tried to defend his Daytona 500 championship but was unsuccessful. Jarrett diced with Wally Dallenbach Jr. (43) and former Daytona 500 winner Derrike Cope (98), who debuted the new Fingerhut colors.
(Right) After a furious battle, Sterling Marlin won his first Winston Cup race — a victory in the "Super Bowl" of the sport, no less!

Testing had shown the tires were fast, but the question the Goodyear-runners asked was whether the Hoosiers would be fast for a full fuel stop, or if the speed of the tires would disappear after a few laps.

At the end of Pole Day, a familiar black and silver Chevrolet sat on the front row. But, to Dale Earnhardt's chagrin, it was the outside of the front row. On the pole was rookie Loy Allen Jr., who had already won the pole for the ARCA race. It was the first time in the history of Daytona's Speedweeks that a driver had won back-to-back poles for the ARCA and NASCAR Winston Cup races — not to mention the fact that the driver in question was a rookie.

During the season-opener, Dale Earnhardt leads a pack that includes Morgan Shepherd and Mark Martin. Despite another strong run, Dale was unable to win the race that has eluded him throughout his illustrious career.

With just the front row locked in — with a Ford on the pole and Earnhardt's Chevrolet alongside — attention turned to the Busch Clash and the first laps turned by the big iron since last November.

The Busch Clash would consist of two 10-lap segments again this year, with the field inverted after the conclusion of the first ten laps. Last year, it had made no difference. Earnhardt blasted everyone in each of the segments to claim the crown. This year, the black Chevrolet appeared destined to repeat history.

Dale blistered his way to the front and led at the halfway mark, and then lined up behind the rest of the field for the rain-delayed start of the second ten. Within minutes, he was back at the front, just behind Ernie

Irvan. Irvan looked strong, but with two laps to go, Jeff Gordon and Brett Bodine drafted past the black cars of Irvan and Earnhardt, leaving the two behind. Earnhardt could handle Irvan and Mark Martin, but Gordon and Bodine were gone. Those two cars touched in the fourth turn, but Gordon pulled ahead to win by a car-length. Gordon went to the winner's circle (after receiving directions on how to get there!), and the Goodyear folks joined the celebration. The Eagles had landed!

In the first Gatorade Twin, Irvan immediately demonstrated why his team was one of the preseason picks to win the whole enchilada. He scorched his way past pole-sitter Loy Allen and fronted the field for the first 27 laps. Ernie once got a little out of shape and had to lift from the throttle to get back under control, but he then continued to lead for the final 10 laps, beating Rusty Wallace by less than a half-second. Goodyear continued its celebration.

This Daytona 500 would mark Earnhardt's 16th try for a victory in the biggest race in the sport. And, despite leading and having a chance late in the race, Dale came up empty once again. However, he had a terrific Speedweeks, landing on the front row for the 500; winning the Busch Series race (for the fifth-straight year!), the first round of the 1994 Dodge IROC Series and the Gatorade Twin 125; and finishing third in the Busch Clash. Still, he hadn't won the big one.

Irvan hadn't either, despite his best efforts and the fact that he had led the race with 19 laps to go. The Havoline Ford driver did finish second, just ahead of Terry Labonte, after drafting with Mark Martin back to the front of the pack with less than two laps to go. But Mark ran out of fuel on the final lap, which handed third back to Labonte.

So who was the winner?

None other than Sterling Marlin, who enjoyed his own Kodak Moment as he circled the track after holding off Irvan by 0.19 of a second. The irony of the victory was not lost on anyone — Marlin had beaten Irvan, who had bolted the Morgan-McClure team last fall to join Robert Yates Racing and take over the Havoline Ford.

Sterling savored the moment. He had waited a long time for his first NASCAR Winston Cup victory. The Daytona 500 was the 279th start of his career — a career during which he had made his NASCAR Winston Cup debut in a car owned by his father in 1976. His dad, former driver Coo Coo Marlin, was on hand and saw the inside of a NASCAR Winston Cup victory lane for the first time as well. Coo Coo had made 165 starts between 1966 and 1980 but had won only a 125-mile qualifying

The second Gatorade Twin rolled out, and for the fifth-straight time, Earnhardt was in victory lane at its conclusion. He had had some work to do, but neither Sterling Marlin nor Jeff Gordon had a real answer. Earnhardt won by a tenth of a second over the Kodak Chevrolet. The Winged Foot troops were stomping up a storm!

The party in Akron continued Friday morning when NASCAR announced that, in the interest of competition, those teams using Hoosiers would be allowed to switch to Goodyears without penalty. Hoosier owner Bob Newton gave the teams his blessing, acknowledging that more work needed to be done on the Hoosiers. Every team switched in preparation for Sunday's season-opener.

In a battle of Pontiacs, Bobby Labonte and Michael Waltrip struggle to match the strength of the Fords and Chevrolets in the Daytona 500.

Rusty Wallace and Mark Martin battle. Wallace was taken out in a multi-car wreck while Martin rolled to a 13th-place finish.

race at Daytona in 1973. At the time, Sterling was working as his right-front tire-changer! Combined, the Marlins were 0-for-443 before Sterling's popular victory.

It wasn't the easiest win: Sterling had to rely on crew member Tim Morgan's prediction that the Kodak Chevrolet could run the final 59 laps, or 147.5 miles, on its final fill-up during the fourth caution at lap 141. Tim was right but not by much. Sterling ran out of fuel coming down pit road headed for victory lane!

Two multi-car wrecks took out several challengers; the first included Rusty Wallace, Kyle Petty, Harry Gant, John Andretti, Jeff Burton, Bobby Hillin, Hut Stricklin and Chuck Bown. Busch Clash winner Jeff Gordon triggered the second by hitting a slick-running Todd Bodine. The resulting crash collected Michael Waltrip, Ted Musgrave, Jimmy Spencer and Brett Bodine. All were lead-lap cars.

While Sterling grinned in victory lane, Earnhardt sat quietly in his transporter. He had fought an ill-handling car

to take the seventh-place finish. He took heart after being reminded that it took Darrell Waltrip 17 tries to finally win the Daytona 500. This was the Big E's 16th attempt. There was still plenty of time, and Dale knew it, even though he didn't care to talk much about it right then.

Finishing behind Labonte was Gordon, who survived the multi-car wrecks. Next were Morgan Shepherd and Greg Sacks, who had a superb showing in his first run with D.K. Ulrich's new team. Ricky Rudd made his team's debut a strong one with an eighth-place finish, while Bill Elliott came home ninth. Kenny Schrader claimed the final top 10 position.

Daytona was finished. Goodyear had beaten back the Hoosier challenge in the most important race of the season. The 500 had rewarded one of the most persistent families in racing: A Marlin had finally won a NASCAR Winston Cup race.

BUSCH CLASH

Loy Allen Jr. was the surprise pole-winner and became the first rookie ever to win the Daytona 500 pole!

Fin. Pos.	Str. Pos.	Car #	Driver	Team	Fin. Pos.	Str. Pos.	Car #	Driver	Team
1	4	4	Sterling Marlin	Kodak Film Chevrolet	22	1	19	Loy Allen	Hooters Ford
2	3	28	Ernie Irvan	Texaco Havoline Ford	23	37	12	Chuck Bown	ReLife Ford
3	9	5	Terry Labonte	Kellogg's Corn Flakes Chevrolet	24	33	90	Bobby Hillin	Heilig-Meyers Ford
4	6	24	Jeff Gordon	DuPont Chevrolet	25	27	71	Dave Marcis	STG/Tork Auto Wipes Chevrolet
5	12	21	Morgan Shepherd	Citgo Ford	26	35	8	Jeff Burton	Raybestos Brakes Ford
6	31	77	Greg Sacks	USAir Ford	27	30	1	Rick Mast	Skoal Classic Ford
7	2	3	Dale Earnhardt	GM Goodwrench Chevrolet	28	32	17	Darrell Waltrip	Western Auto Chevrolet
8	20	10	Ricky Rudd	Tide Ford	29	17	97	Chad Little	Tracy Lawrence Ford
9	8	11	Bill Elliott	Budweiser Ford	30	40	95	Jeremy Mayfield	Shoney's Ford
10	13	25	Ken Schrader	Kodiak Chevrolet	31	14	30	Michael Waltrip	Pennzoil Pontiac
11	39	7	Geoff Bodine	Exide Batteries Ford	32	10	26	Brett Bodine	Quaker State Ford
12	23	40	Bobby Hamilton	Kendall Pontiac	33	38	23	Hut Stricklin	Smokin' Joe's Ford
13	7	6	Mark Martin	Valvoline Ford	34	36	33	Harry Gant	Skoal Bandit Chevrolet
14	22	15	Lake Speed	Quality Care Ford	35	41	18	Dale Jarrett	Interstate Batteries Chevrolet
15	25	55	Jimmy Hensley	Petron Plus Ford	36	11	75	Todd Bodine	Factory Stores of America Ford
16	42	22	Bobby Labonte	Maxwell House Coffee Pontiac	37	21	27	Jimmy Spencer	McDonald's Ford
17	18	43	Wally Dallenbach	STP Pontiac	38	24	16	Ted Musgrave	The Family Channel Ford
18	34	9	Joe Ruttman	Melling Engine Parts Ford	39	26	42	Kyle Petty	Mello Yello Pontiac
19	28	80	Jimmy Horton	Hover Motorsports Ford	40	19	54	Robert Pressley	Manheim Auctions Chevrolet
20	29	32	Dick Trickle	ATS Wood Recycling Chevrolet	41	5	2	Rusty Wallace	Miller Genuine Draft Ford
21	16	98	Derrike Cope	Fingerhut Ford	42	15	14	John Andretti	Financial World Chevrolet

GOODWRENCH 500

**NORTH CAROLINA
MOTOR SPEEDWAY**

FEBRUARY 27, 1994

Following a bout of food poisoning (caused by a convenience store hot dog) and a visit to the Governor's Mansion in Tennessee, Daytona 500 winner Sterling Marlin arrived at Rockingham in the highest of spirits. Ernie Irvan may have finished second and led the most laps at The Beach, but Sterling was now parked at the front of the line in the garage. He and Irvan shared the NASCAR Winston Cup point lead, each with 180 points. For the moment at least, the Kodak Chevrolet was amidst the rest of the big guns in Cup racing.

The previous week had been a heady experience for Marlin, but this was a new week, and the Goodwrench 500 at Frank Wilson's North Carolina Motor Speedway paid exactly the same number of championship points as the Daytona 500 had the week before.

It was time to get back to business.

After factoring in their Daytona finishes, some of the competitors who were expected to challenge for the championship instead faced an uphill battle in the standings. Rusty Wallace and Kyle Petty were at the bottom of the list, and each was more than 130 points behind the leader. Jimmy Spencer and the Mac Attack were behind, too, along with Dale Jarrett, Harry Gant, Brett and Todd Bodine and Darrell and Michael Waltrip. Each driver had paid the price for being in the wrong place at the wrong time at Daytona.

(Top) Rusty Wallace held off Morgan Shepherd and the rest of the field for his first victory lane appearance of the young season. (Right) Rick Mast tries to gain ground on Brett Bodine's Quaker State Ford.

(Top) Darrell Waltrip's Chevrolet leads Steve Grissom's Chevrolet and the Fords of Derrike Cope and Morgan Shepherd in Goodwrench 500 action. (Right) The fine-tuning of cars at race tracks sometimes requires that crew members become acrobats.

Goodyear had won the first round of the tire battle, but Hoosiers were back — after qualifying had been completed, Bob Newton was grinning once again. Lead Hoosier driver Geoff Bodine had turned the fastest qualifying lap and slapped his Exide Ford on the pole. Still, no one knew what to expect from the Purple H tires because they had yet to run a NASCAR Winston Cup race.

The first 14 drivers on the grid for Sunday's race all had broken the track record. With the renewed competition between the two brands of tires, qualifying had taken on new importance as the first competition of the weekend. Teams had never worried very much about qualifying, but with new teams entering the sport and more teams than spots available in the field, the choice of tires and set-ups had never been more important.

Mark Martin took the outside of the front row, less than two-one-hundredths of a second behind, and proved that the Hoosier edge was slight indeed. Jeff Gordon and Brett Bodine made up the second row, with Ted Musgrave and Ernie Irvan behind them. Kyle Petty and Bill Elliott were in the fourth row, and Darrell Waltrip and Bobby Hamilton (who was sporting Kendall Oil colors for the second-straight race as Felix Sabates' second-team driver) completed the top 10.

After the first round, crowd favorites Rusty Wallace and Dale Earnhardt were 15th and 19th, respectively — safely in the field, but with some work to do on Sunday. They were among the fortunate. Jeremy Mayfield, Ward Burton, T.W. Taylor, Indy 500 winner Danny Sullivan (with yet another new team), Jerry Hill, NASCAR Winston West champ Rick Carelli and James Hylton all had to find something else to do Sunday. They failed to make the field. And Dale Jarrett, fourth in the final standings in 1993, along with Daytona 500 pole-sitter Loy Allen, were forced to take provisionals to get into the Goodwrench 500 field.

As the field rolled off the line, a misty-eyed group gathered high above the start/finish line in the Unocal suite. The Goodwrench 500 marked the final event that Dick Dolan, Unocal's automotive event manager, would orchestrate for the oil company. Dolan, who had been the only person to hold that position at Pure Oil Company and then Unocal (after it merged with Pure in 1965), would retire the following day. Since 1952, when Pure became involved with NASCAR racing, Dolan had been "The Man." For more than four decades he and his wife, Betty, had been fixtures at every track on the tour. The contributions he made to the sport throughout his long career have touched every competitor, every track management official and every media member. Although he will no longer be involved in the sport day-to-day, he will continue with Unocal 76 as a consultant.

The drivers could not have produced a better sendoff for Dolan. Geoff Bodine led the field to the green flag from the inside of the front row (his first pole as a team owner and the first for the former Alan Kulwicki team

"So, there we were — me and the Hulkster — in a Steel Cage Match. I just throttled him to win the World Television championship!" Dale seems unimpressed with Michael Waltrip's description as they head for the start of the Goodwrench 500.

25

since 1992), but it immediately became apparent that Goodyear was the proper choice of the day at Rockingham. Bodine lasted only four laps at the front before Martin decided enough was enough and left the black and blue Ford in the dust. For more than 100 laps, Mark battled first with a hard-charging Wallace and then with Sterling Marlin, who proved that the strength of his Kodak Chevrolet at Daytona wasn't a fluke. Martin faded from contention when he received a mismatched set of tires late in the race. He was forced to pit and then lost a lap when the last caution came out with 22 laps to go. The Valvoline Ford driver did finish fourth, however.

Once Wallace arrived at the front, the black Ford became difficult to dislodge. Rusty was determined to prove that his switch to the Blue Oval for 1994 was the right decision. He dominated the field over the final three-quarters of the race, leading 346 of 492 laps, and held off a challenge from Marlin for the victory. Sterling, more than five seconds behind Rusty, was mirror-driving to maintain his second-place position. A determined Rick Mast dogged Sterling's every move but couldn't find his

way past the Kodak Chevrolet in the final laps.

For Irvan, a hard-earned fifth place was worth a smile. His Ford had not handled well for most of the race and had lost a cylinder with some 50 laps to go. Still, he managed to finish ahead of Brett Bodine and Earnhardt. Earnhardt led late in the race before a loose lug nut forced a green-flag stop with 10 laps remaining.

Kyle Petty, Ken Schrader and Michael Waltrip completed the top 10, and although Darrell Waltrip finished 23rd, he considered it a victory of sorts. Darrell had spent three days between Daytona and Rockingham in the hospital, battling a kidney infection. To be able to fight his way to the finish at one of the toughest, most grueling races of the season put a testy smile on the old warhorse. He had suffered through flat tires and an ignition problem but still made it to the finish.

When the teams loaded their charges after the second race of the year, Sterling sat alone at the top of the point

Ernie Irvan streaks past Bill Elliott's mangled Ford at North Carolina Motor Speedway.

table. Ernie was 20 points behind and Dale had moved from sixth to third.

But the big bite had been taken by the race winner. With his dominant performance (and his third consecutive Rockingham victory) Rusty had out-run the opposition and moved from 41st to 13th in the standings.

The importance of pit stops and solid work by the crew at every race on the circuit cannot be overstated. Morgan McClure Racing jackman Robert Larkins works his way around front tire-changer Mark Prater as they pit Sterling Marlin's Kodak Chevrolet.

Fin. Pos.	Str. Pos.	Car #	Driver	Team	Fin. Pos.	Str. Pos.	Car #	Driver	Team
1	15	2	Rusty Wallace	Miller Genuine Draft Ford	22	33	55	Jimmy Hensley	Petron Plus Ford
2	21	4	Sterling Marlin	Kodak Film Chevrolet	23	9	17	Darrell Waltrip	Western Auto Chevrolet
3	16	1	Rick Mast	Skoal Classic Ford	24	35	14	John Andretti	Financial World Chevrolet
4	2	6	Mark Martin	Valvoline Ford	25	25	12	Chuck Bown	ReLife Ford
5	6	28	Ernie Irvan	Texaco Havoline Ford	26	24	23	Hut Stricklin	Smokin' Joe's Ford
6	4	26	Brett Bodine	Quaker State Ford	27	22	43	Wally Dallenbach	STP Pontiac
7	19	3	Dale Earnhardt	GM Goodwrench Chevrolet	28	30	77	Greg Sacks	USAir Ford
8	7	42	Kyle Petty	Mello Yello Pontiac	29	32	98	Derrike Cope	Fingerhut Ford
9	13	25	Ken Schrader	Kodiak Chevrolet	30	12	29	Steve Grissom	Diamond Ridge Chevrolet
10	31	30	Michael Waltrip	Pennzoil Pontiac	31	38	52	Mike Skinner	NAPA Ford
11	34	10	Ricky Rudd	Tide Ford	32	3	24	Jeff Gordon	DuPont Chevrolet
12	26	27	Jimmy Spencer	McDonald's Ford	33	18	90	Bobby Hillin	Heilig-Meyers Ford
13	5	16	Ted Musgrave	The Family Channel Ford	34	14	75	Todd Bodine	Factory Stores of America Ford
14	29	32	Dick Trickle	ATS Wood Recycling Chevrolet	35	40	71	Dave Marcis	Terramite Const. Eq. Chevrolet
15	1	7	Geoff Bodine	Exide Batteries Ford	36	23	41	Joe Nemechek	Meineke Mufflers Chevrolet
16	11	21	Morgan Shepherd	Citgo Ford	37	17	33	Harry Gant	Skoal Bandit Chevrolet
17	27	5	Terry Labonte	Kellogg's Corn Flakes Chevrolet	38	10	40	Bobby Hamilton	Kendall Pontiac
18	41	18	Dale Jarrett	Interstate Batteries Chevrolet	39	8	11	Bill Elliott	Budweiser Ford
19	20	22	Bobby Labonte	Maxwell House Coffee Pontiac	40	42	19	Loy Allen	Hooters Ford
20	39	8	Jeff Burton	Raybestos Brakes Ford	41	36	9	Rick Bickle	Melling Engine Parts Ford
21	37	15	Lake Speed	Quality Care Ford	42	28	47	Billy Standridge	Johnson Racing Ford

PONTIAC EXCITEMENT 400

RICHMOND
INTERNATIONAL RACEWAY

MARCH 6, 1994

As the teams assembled at Paul Sawyer's mini-superspeedway for the Pontiac Excitement 400, Bobby Hamilton and Felix Sabates created a little excitement of their own. Felix's Daytona gamble (listing Kendall Motor Oil as the primary sponsor on Hamilton's car even though the Pennsylvania oil company had only a limited associate sponsor deal at the

(Top) During the Pontiac Excitement 400, Terry Labonte's Kellogg's crew finishes the right side during a pit stop. (Right) Greg Sacks heads up the field at Richmond.

time) had made the difference. Felix and Bobby announced on the eve of qualifying that Kendall would be the team's primary sponsor for the remainder of the season.

Felix and Bobby had plenty to grin about, but the folks in the Hoosier camp were wearing confident looks as well. They had brought a "cantilevered" tire, used for years on short tracks around the country, to NASCAR Winston Cup, hoping the wider tread-width would give the Purple H drivers a bigger contact patch and more adhesion to the .75-mile track's surface.

During qualifying, however, the top 10 drivers eschewed the Hoosier offering and put Goodyear Eagles on the first five rows of the grid! It was the first Goodyear pole of the season.

With 45 cars entered, the tire choice became critical. Several drivers knew, after looking around the garage Friday, that unless they cranked it up, they would be watching the Sunday race on television.

Chuck Bown, driving Bobby Allison's Ford, was the early qualifying leader. He set the pace until Mark Martin ran his lap in the Valvoline Ford. Mark pushed Chuck into the second spot and then watched his teammate, Ted Musgrave, win his first career Winston Cup pole with a lap nearly a tenth of a second faster!

It was the first time Jack Roush's two team cars had been on the front row since he had entered NASCAR Winston Cup racing and the second time this season that a driver had won his first Winston Cup pole (Loy Allen Jr. had been the quickest at Daytona).

Behind Ted, Mark and Chuck were Rick Mast, Michael

(Bottom / Right) Bobby Labonte tries to avoid
Dick Trickle's wrecked Chevrolet at Richmond.
Morgan Shepherd and Bobby Hillin (90) take
the low route, and Lake Speed (15) takes
evasive action as well. After the yellow flag
came out, Trickle took a look at the damage.

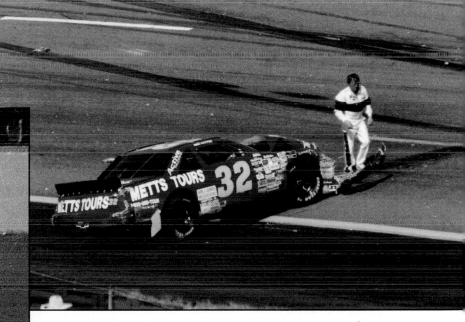

Waltrip (in his best qualifying effort since Dover in 1992,
51 races ago) and Daytona 500 winner Sterling Marlin.
Filling out the top 10 were Ernie Irvan, Jeff Gordon, Dale
Earnhardt and Jimmy Spencer. Earnhardt had failed to
make the field for the Busch Grand National race for the
first time in his NASCAR BGN and Winston Cup career.
He was not about to miss the "big show!"

Joe Nemechek was the first Hoosier qualifier, claiming
the inside of the sixth row, with Rusty Wallace alongside.
But there were some long faces in the garage area
following the conclusion of second round qualifying.
Ricky Rudd had made the field as the final qualifier in
34th place, and Hamilton and Bobby Hillin had taken
provisional positions based on the 1993 car owner points
used until the Atlanta race. Terry Labonte was forced to
take the former NASCAR Winston Cup Champion's provisional and started shotgun on the field.

Wally Dallenbach was out in the cold, but he was not
alone. Others headed home to watch the race were: Billy
Standridge, Hut Stricklin, Daytona 500 pole-sitter Loy
Allen, Rich Bickle, Winston West Champion Rick
Carelli, Mike Wallace, Dave Marcis and I.W. Taylor.

R.J. Reynolds and Travis Carter Racing immediately
cut a deal with Bobby Allison and Chuck Bown to carry
Smokin' Joe's colors in Sunday's 400-lapper, and the team
was hastily provided with sweatshirts and other items of
apparel from the souvenir trailer.

After the green flag flew Sunday afternoon, the first
quarter of the race was a battle among pole-sitter
Musgrave, Martin, Mast and Earnhardt, but Irvan ran in
the top five, getting a feel for what the track had to offer.
On lap 106, Ernie put the Havoline Ford at the front
when Jeff Gordon headed for pit lane during green flag
stops. From that point on, the Richmond race was a

31

Dale Jarrett (18), Jeff Gordon (24) and Darrell Waltrip (17) waged their own private struggle during the Richmond race.

battle between black Fords, with either Irvan or Rusty Wallace fronting the field for all but 10 of the remaining 290-plus laps.

This race was the last one Davey Allison had won with the Robert Yates team, and no one had forgotten. Twice in the final 50 laps, the Havoline team responded by getting Irvan out of the pits first, beating the vaunty Miller team at its own game. Both times, Ernie used the 17-second stops to his advantage and pulled away from Wallace.

By the time the checkered fell, Irvan had pulled away to a 1.7-second margin over the Miller Ford, and after winning his first race of the season, Ernie had plenty to smile about. He had defended the race title won

Rusty Wallace's Miller team performed to their own standards and pitted Wallace in fine style throughout the day.

last year by the team and, in the process, had taken over the NASCAR Winston Cup point lead. Gordon ran a strong race to finish third, and Earnhardt finished a very solid fourth, driving what he called a "third- or fourth-place car today."

Wallace also had reason to smile following his runner-up finish. It was the ninth-straight short track race in which Rusty had finished either first or second, and it moved him from 13th to eighth in the point standings. But he wasn't the only one streaking up the point ladder. Kyle Petty finished fifth and moved from 21st to 13th.

Behind Petty came Martin, finishing sixth after encountering throttle linkage problems while running in the top three near half-distance. Rick

Mast backed up his strong qualifying run with a seventh-place finish, and Brett Bodine was eighth. In a superb showing, Terry Labonte finished as the final car on the lead lap, taking his Kellogg's Chevrolet all the way from 37th position at the start to ninth. Dale Jarrett, after having to use provisionals the first two races, started 22nd and finished 10th. Darrell Waltrip, in 16th place, was the highest-ranked Hoosier driver, finishing two laps down.

With 53 points in hand after the first three races, Ernie and the Robert Yates team headed for Atlanta. Earnhardt, Marlin and Martin were tightly bunched behind him, and Rusty also had begun his run.

The Budweiser girls were one of the pit road highlights at Richmond!

Fin. Pos.	Str. Pos.	Car #	Driver	Team	Fin. Pos.	Str. Pos.	Car #	Driver	Team
1	7	28	Ernie Irvan	Texaco Havoline Ford	20	25	8	Jeff Burton	Raybestos Brakes Ford
2	12	2	Rusty Wallace	Miller Genuine Draft Ford	21	11	41	Joe Nemechek	Meineke Mufflers Chevrolet
3	8	24	Jeff Gordon	DuPont Chevrolet	22	10	27	Jimmy Spencer	McDonald's Ford
4	9	3	Dale Earnhardt	GM Goodwrench Chevrolet	23	15	29	Steve Grissom	Diamond Ridge Chevrolet
5	19	42	Kyle Petty	Mello Yello Pontiac	24	31	22	Bobby Labonte	Maxwell House Coffee Pontiac
6	2	6	Mark Martin	Valvoline Ford	25	14	75	Todd Bodine	Factory Stores of America Ford
7	4	1	Rick Mast	Skoal Classic Ford	26	36	90	Bobby Hillin	Heilig-Meyers Ford
8	13	26	Brett Bodine	Quaker State Ford	27	18	95	Jeremy Mayfield	Shoney's Inn Ford
9	37	5	Terry Labonte	Kellogg's Corn Flakes Chevrolet	28	21	77	Greg Sacks	USAir Ford
10	22	18	Dale Jarrett	Interstate Batteries Chevrolet	29	33	98	Derrike Cope	Fingerhut Ford
11	16	25	Ken Schrader	Kodiak Chevrolet	30	24	14	John Andretti	Financial World Chevrolet
12	26	11	Bill Elliott	Budweiser Ford	31	5	30	Michael Waltrip	Pennzoil Pontiac
13	1	16	Ted Musgrave	The Family Channel Ford	32	17	7	Geoff Bodine	Exide Batteries Ford
14	30	15	Lake Speed	Quality Care Ford	33	35	40	Bobby Hamilton	Kendall Pontiac
15	32	21	Morgan Shepherd	Citgo Ford	34	28	33	Harry Gant	Skoal Bandit Chevrolet
16	27	17	Darrell Waltrip	Western Auto Chevrolet	35	29	31	Ward Burton	Hardee's Chevrolet
17	3	12	Chuck Bown	Smokin' Joe's Ford	36	23	55	Jimmy Hensley	Petron Plus Ford
18	34	10	Ricky Rudd	Tide Ford	37	20	32	Dick Trickle	Mett's Tours Chevrolet
19	6	4	Sterling Marlin	Kodak Film Chevrolet					

PUROLATOR 500

ATLANTA MOTOR SPEEDWAY

MARCH 13, 1994

In the few days between Richmond and Atlanta, several teams experienced the winds of change. The day following the Richmond race, Bobby Hillin resigned his ride with Junie Donlavey's Heilig-Meyers team citing "philosophical differences" with the popular car owner regarding the "Furniture Fords." Donlavey responded by hiring Mike Wallace from the Busch Grand National ranks, which enabled Mike to run for Maxx Rookie of the Year honors in NASCAR Winston Cup.

T. W. Taylor, unable to get his team's Ford into the field of any of the first three races of the season, fired himself as driver and hired Curtis Markham

(Top) During one of Ricky Rudd's pit stops at Atlanta, jackman John Bryan puts his all into his work as Randy Usher arrives with tires. The rear tire-changer on the Tide crew is Keith Koldsbaek and the front tire-changer is Bill Miller.
(Right) Victory lane is the perfect place to end the Atlanta race according to winner Ernie Irvan. Ernie shares the limelight with Miss Winston.

for the Atlanta race. Rich Bickle was told he would be the "permanent" driver for the limited schedule of races the Harry Melling Ford team planned to run in 1994. P.J. Jones had opened the season in the car. Jeff Purvis was now behind the wheel of the Country Time Lemonade Chevrolet.

After eight years of boasting the red and white Motorcraft Parts and Service colors, the spring race at Atlanta

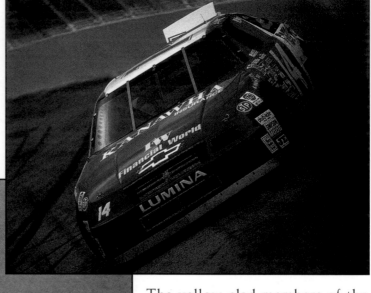

changed its stripes. Purolator took over title sponsorship, and the 328-lap race at general manager Ed Clark's 1.5-mile track became the Purolator 500. New signage and promotion greeted the teams upon their arrival, and all were delighted to see the longtime NASCAR sponsor return to the sport.

For one team, the weekend at Atlanta held no joy.

The yellow-clad members of the Pennzoil team carried a very personal grief to the track. Team co-owner Chuck Rider's wife, Pat, had lost a long and gallant battle with illness that Wednesday. Driver Michael Waltrip arrived at the track Friday after serving as a pall-bearer earlier that morning.

But there was work to be done for qualifying, and Loy Allen, continuing his pattern of "feast or famine," went out late in the session and won the pole with his Hoosier-shod Hooters Ford. In the process, Allen also set a new track record. It was Allen's second pole of the season, and a treat after he had failed to qualify the previous week at Richmond.

It was the fourth consecutive pole of the young season for a Ford. Allen's pole also had given Hoosier a 3-1 edge over Goodyear with regard to the fastest qualifying laps of the year. Alongside Allen, and giving those equipped with Goodyear tires reason to fret, was Geoff Bodine, who completed a Hoosier front row with his Exide Ford.

Terry Labonte and Mark Martin claimed the second row on

In the early going at Atlanta, Bobby Labonte heads the pack of cars that includes Ernie Irvan, Ricky Rudd and Bobby Hamilton.

Goodyears. Joe Nemechek (Hoosiers) was fifth-fastest, and Bickle (Goodyears) was a surprising sixth-fastest. NASCAR Winston Cup point leader Ernie Irvan and rookie contender Ward Burton took care of the fourth row. Chuck Bown continued his good qualifying performances to grab the ninth spot, just a tick faster than Greg Sacks. Harry Gant and Rusty Wallace made up the sixth row, and Dale Earnhardt, second in the point standings, would start from 16th place Sunday. Markham surprised many by not just making the field for Taylor's team, but qualifying 18th.

Jimmy Hensley and Mike Wallace took the provisional spots for the race. Jeremy Mayfield, Billy Standridge, Jim Sauter and Jimmy Horton were sent home to watch the race. Also missing the event were Buddy Baker (wrecked the Moroso Ford in Friday qualifying), Wally Dallenbach (the second-straight time Petty Enterprises hadn't made the field), Indy 500 winner Danny Sullivan (failed in his second try to get into a Cup race), and NASCAR Winston West champ Rick Carelli (unable, for the fourth time, to get into a 1994 NASCAR Winston Cup event).

Part of the weekend festivities at Atlanta included a sneak preview of NASCARWorld, an interactive "theme park on wheels" devoted to the sport of NASCAR Winston Cup racing. The exhibit would be open for visitors to Indianapolis for the Brickyard 400 in August and would include exhibits and activities enabling fans to see and participate in different aspects of the sport. Modeled after the "NFL Experience" and the NBA's "Fan Jam," NASCARWorld allows "hands-on" participation of spectators.

Sunday morning's talk in the garage area was about tires — specifically, whether or not the edge Hoosier had shown in qualifying would last during the race. No matter whom one asked, they had a theory about either Goodyear or Hoosier. Finally, one crew chief threw up his hands and said, "Look, you're the 500th person who's asked me that this morning. Let's just go race and find out!"

He got his wish.

Geoff Bodine flashed to the pole early, and then Irvan made his way to the front. But by the time a fourth of the race was run, a surprising face was leading the pack. Once Jeff Burton got to the front he seemingly led at will, and by the time the race began its second half, the blue and white Raybestos Ford was clearly the class of the field. Burton ran away and hid, building a lead of 18 seconds (at Atlanta, about a half-lap) and no one had anything for him. But then Lady Luck decided to change seats, and Burton was unable to dominate after his car's previously superior handling faded.

Mark Martin was caught in the pits when a yellow came out during a green-flag stop, and the Valvoline Ford driver lost a lap he was never able to regain due to the dominance of Irvan and Burton. Terry Labonte, an

Lake Speed finished sixth in Bud Moore's Quality Care Ford at Bill Elliott's home track.

early leader, twice had left-side tire problems due to a malfunctioning air gun, Sterling Marlin overheated and Rusty Wallace was black-flagged on the 30th lap for a broken air duct that required that the right-side window be replaced on his Ford. Earnhardt struggled throughout the day and was three laps down at the conclusion.

At the end, the only car able to challenge Irvan was perennial Atlanta contender Morgan Shepherd, who quietly and effectively took the Wood Brothers' Ford through its paces the entire day. Morgan battled Irvan during the closing laps but just didn't have enough to

make a run at the Havoline Ford. Ernie was in front by .35 of a second at the conclusion of the Purolator 500.

A surprising third was Darrell Waltrip, who had called his Western Auto Chevrolet "junk" after his 40th-fastest qualifying time — just barely enough to get into the field without a provisional. But in the race, Darrell found the right combination and led three times — a fine way for the three-time champion to celebrate his 600th career start.

Behind Waltrip came Jeff Burton, the final car on the lead lap. Not surprisingly, Burton was disappointed after losing the handle that had allowed him to dominate earlier in the race. Martin was fifth, ahead of Lake Speed and Greg Sacks. Jeff Gordon, Ricky Rudd and Jimmy Spencer completed the top 10. Wallace was classified 24th, taking a hit in the point race.

Irvan had given Ford and Goodyear another win and had boosted his point margin to 101 (after four races) in the process. Martin moved to second place in the standings, displacing Earnhardt, while Morgan climbed to fourth. Rusty slid to 11th in the standings and now trailed Irvan by 214 as the teams headed for Darlington.

The Goodwrench pit crew works its magic under the watchful eye of a NASCAR official.

Fin. Pos.	Str. Pos.	Car #	Driver	Team	Fin. Pos.	Str. Pos.	Car #	Driver	Team
1	7	28	Ernie Irvan	Texaco Havoline Ford	22	1	19	Loy Allen	Hooters Ford
2	14	21	Morgan Shepherd	Citgo Ford	23	32	30	Michael Waltrip	Pennzoil Pontiac
3	40	17	Darrell Waltrip	Western Auto Chevrolet	24	12	2	Rusty Wallace	Miller Genuine Draft Ford
4	13	8	Jeff Burton	Raybestos Brakes Ford	25	23	4	Sterling Marlin	Kodak Film Chevrolet
5	4	6	Mark Martin	Valvoline Ford	26	37	1	Rick Mast	Skoal Classic Ford
6	34	15	Lake Speed	Quality Care Ford	27	42	90	Mike Wallace	Heilig-Meyers Ford
7	10	77	Greg Sacks	USAir Ford	28	20	32	Dick Trickle	Active Trucking Chevrolet
8	17	24	Jeff Gordon	DuPont Chevrolet	29	41	55	Jimmy Hensley	Petron Plus Ford
9	22	10	Ricky Rudd	Tide Ford	30	11	33	Harry Gant	Skoal Bandit Chevrolet
10	25	27	Jimmy Spencer	McDonald's Ford	31	15	26	Brett Bodine	Quaker State Ford
11	35	16	Ted Musgrave	The Family Channel Ford	32	21	11	Bill Elliott	Budweiser Ford
12	16	3	Dale Earnhardt	GM Goodwrench Chevrolet	33	19	75	Todd Bodine	Factory Stores of America Ford
13	27	42	Kyle Petty	Mello Yello Pontiac	34	29	98	Derrike Cope	Fingerhut Ford
14	3	5	Terry Labonte	Kellogg's Corn Flakes Chevrolet	35	36	18	Dale Jarrett	Interstate Batteries Chevrolet
15	30	22	Bobby Labonte	Maxwell House Coffee Pontiac	36	38	71	Dave Marcis	STG Chevrolet
16	24	25	Ken Schrader	Kodiak Chevrolet	37	6	9	Rich Bickle	Melling Engine Parts Ford
17	39	23	Hut Stricklin	Smokin' Joe's Ford	38	2	7	Geoff Bodine	Exide Batteries Ford
18	5	41	Joe Nemechek	Meineke Mufflers Chevrolet	39	18	02	Curtis Markham	Children's Miracle Network Ford
19	33	40	Bobby Hamilton	Kendall Pontiac	40	8	31	Ward Burton	Hardee's Chevrolet
20	31	29	Steve Grissom	Diamond Ridge Chevrolet	41	9	12	Chuck Bown	Crown Fiber Ford
21	28	51	Jeff Purvis	Country Time Chevrolet	42	26	14	John Andretti	Freedom Village USA Chevrolet

TranSouth Financial 400

DARLINGTON
RACEWAY

MARCH 27, 1994

As the NASCAR Winston Cup teams unloaded at Darlington, Sterling Marlin regaled those in the garage area with tales of his family's DisneyWorld adventures. He had been the grand marshal at a parade honoring the Daytona 500 winner. While some were listening to Sterling's stories about Mickey and Goofy, the Diamond Ridge team and driver Steve Grissom were focused on more serious matters: The team was without the services of general manager Eddie Jones and crew chief Marc Reno. Both had left the team after a personnel shake-up.

(Top) Morgan Shepherd struggled throughout the day at the spring Darlington race; he finished 32nd. (Right) Harry Gant had hoped to continue his success at Darlington but had to settle for an eighth-place finish at the conclusion of the 400-miler.

Darlington had a new look. The Tyler Tower, located on the backstretch, provided an additional 8,000 seats and was open for business. Eventually, hospitality suites will be installed above the seats, a new press box and media center will be constructed, and the current backstretch will become the frontstretch when the track is "flopped." This is all expected to be completed in time for the 1996 running of the TranSouth 400.

This year marked the spring race's return to its 400-mile length for the first time since the Rebel 400 was bumped to 500 miles in 1973. Everyone, including sponsor TranSouth, expected the shorter length to result in even more competition, and in anticipation of greater things to come, the company announced it would extend its sponsorship of the event to 1997.

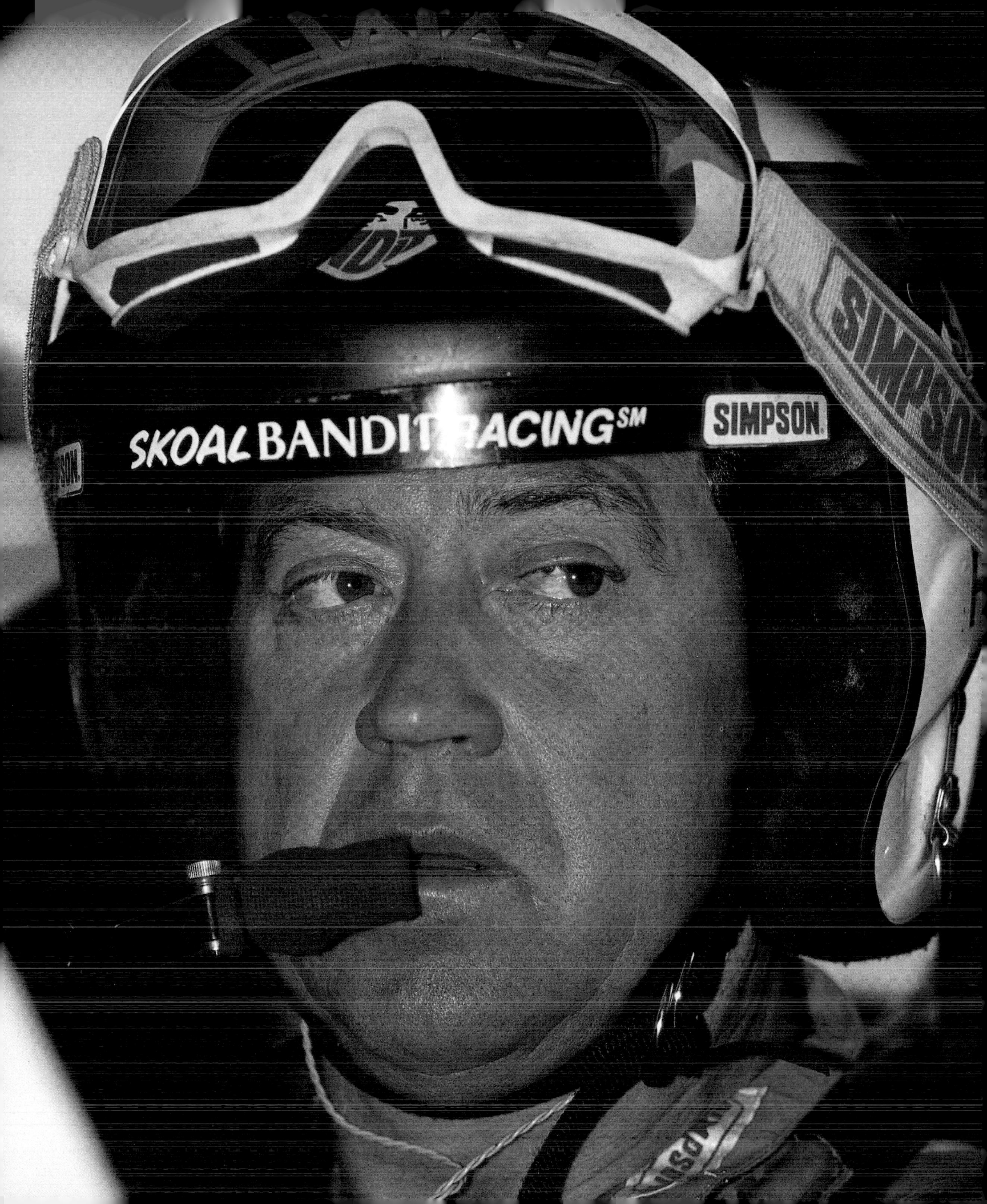
SKOAL BANDIT RACING SM
SIMPSON
SIMPSON

Goodyear had done its homework in tire testing at Darlington, and the Eagles brought to the venerable track proved to be awesome in qualifying. Darlington's 30-second barrier was eclipsed for the first time in history. In fact, the tires were so good that 12 cars had run under the magical mark by the end of qualifying.

If the tires were awesome, so was the pole-winner. Bill Elliott, driving what he called a "perfect lap," was the best of the 26 drivers to shatter the track record; he plopped his Budweiser Ford on the pole with a lap of 29.704 seconds. He had to run a perfect lap — Marlin,

At the conclusion of second-round qualifying, Todd Bodine found himself forced to take a provisional to get into the field. Curtis Markham, Billy Standridge, Bob Schact, H.B. Bailey, Norm Benning and Andy Belmont headed home. Also loading their trailers were NASCAR Winston West champ Rick Carelli, who failed to make the field for the fifth time, and Loy Allen, who continued his trend of either winning the pole or not making the field. (He had failed to qualify at Rockingham but used a provisional to get in.)

The smart money for Sunday was on Earnhardt,

Rusty Wallace returns to competition at Darlington with the gas catch-can stuck on the overflow tube. He returned to pit road to have it removed on the next lap.

with what he called a "real stump-puller" stuffed under his Kodak Chevrolet's hood, notched a lap at 29.751 seconds. He would start alongside Elliott. Mark Martin and Chuck Bown made up the second row with Brett Bodine and Kenny Schrader starting right behind. Geoff Bodine was the only Hoosier-clad runner in the top 20 at the end of the first day; he would start alongside eighth-fastest qualifier Rusty Wallace. Dale Earnhardt and Rick Mast made up the fifth row. NASCAR Winston Cup point leader Ernie Irvan was 11th-fastest, just ahead of Derrike Cope, in Cale Yarborough's Ford.

despite the fact that the driver of the black Chevrolet had yet to win a race in 1994. Dale had won five TranSouth 500s and three Mountain Dew Southern 500s in his career and had triumphed in seven of his last 16 starts at the 1.366-mile track. Goodyear's tires were fast but susceptible to excessive wear on the gritty Darlington surface, so Earnhardt had made some chassis changes Sunday morning, giving up a little handling for less tire wear. It proved to be a key decision for the day.

For the longest time, the race looked like it was Rusty Wallace's to win, but following a green-flag pit stop, he

(Above) Ernie Irvan was one of the front-runners throughout the day: Here he battles with a tenacious Rick Mast. At the finish, Ernie's Texaco Ford was classified sixth.

headed out with loose left side lug nuts. His crew, usually the best on pit road, had made a mistake: They had loosened the left-side lugs in preparation for a four-tire stop, but Rusty had taken just right-sides. The mistake dropped him from the lead to 10th place. Wallace clawed back to the front, climbing to fourth place before he cut a tire and smacked the wall. It cost him 75 laps to repair the damage. He was classified 33rd.

A mistake by Irvan's crew also cost him a chance to win. More than seven crew members were over the wall during a pit stop on lap 221 — the subsequent stop-and-go penalty put an end to his chances.

Sterling Marlin led early but was forced to retire when his Kodak Chevrolet developed engine problems.

(Top) It was the first victory of the young season for Dale Earnhardt, and his pleasure was obvious after he emerged from the Goodwrench Chevrolet. (Left) Dale Earnhardt and Rusty Wallace staged a fabulous mid-race battle for the Darlington victory; Earnhardt emerged victorious.

He did, however, fight his way back to a sixth-place finish, salvaging as much as he could from the situation.

A shrewd Earnhardt was now in command of the race, and he pressed his advantage. Goodyear's supply of 1,850 tires was depleted by the near-constant pit stops, so NASCAR announced on lap 163 that teams could switch to Hoosiers if they wished, as long as they used four tires of the same brand.

All the fuss didn't bother Earnhardt. He led 166 laps and had pushed his advantage to more than seven seconds over runner-up Mark Martin by the conclusion of the 293 laps. Martin was happy with his second place but would have been more delighted to stand in victory lane. He had already beaten the NASCAR Busch series field and also won his first Dodge IROC series race during the weekend. The second-place finish kept him from sweeping the events.

Pole-sitter Elliott finished third, and Dale Jarrett had his best finish of the season, coming home fourth. Lake Speed ran a steady race on a track he loves and brought Bud

Moore's Quality Care Ford home fifth, and Schrader finished behind Irvan in seventh. Harry Gant had a solid run to eighth place, just ahead of Ricky Rudd and Ted Musgrave.

Earnhardt had made the right chassis choice and shown Darlington the respect it demands. His reward was his ninth victory at the track, just one win less than David Pearson's all-time record of ten wins. More importantly, it was the fifth time in his career that Darlington had provided his first win of the season. Earnhardt was quick to point out that in four of those five years, he had emerged as the NASCAR Winston Cup champion at the end of the season.

Bill Elliott took the Budweiser Ford to the Pole and got his first top five finish.

WALTER D. "RED" TYLER

Just a week before the running of the TranSouth 400, the sport of NASCAR Winston Cup racing lost one of its pioneers, Walter D. "Red" Tyler. Red, the former president of Darlington International Raceway and one of the most popular figures in the sport, died of a heart attack at the age of 73. Red began work with Darlington in 1954. He was the track association's vice president from 1967-83 and its president from 1983 until his retirement in 1989. He attended The Citadel and Presbyterian College and was the president and co-owner of Tyler Plywood in Florence, SC. He had served as the chairman of the South Carolina Parole Board and was a recipient of South Carolina's highest honor, "The Order of the Palmetto," presented by the governor of the state.

Just five days before his death, Darlington's new high-rise grandstand, The Tyler Tower, was dedicated in the former track president's honor. He will be missed not only by his wife, Marjorie, his daughter Nancy McKay, his son Walter D. III and his brother, Dan, but also by every competitor and media member. All will remember Red's molasses-slow drawl and quick wit. He was a man who always had at least four new jokes to tell and a man who loved Darlington International Raceway more than any other.

Fin. Pos.	Str. Pos.	Car #	Driver	Team	Fin. Pos.	Str. Pos.	Car #	Driver	Team
1	9	3	Dale Earnhardt	GM Goodwrench Chevrolet	22	41	75	Todd Bodine	Factory Stores of America Ford
2	3	6	Mark Martin	Valvoline Ford	23	31	9	Rich Bickle	Melling Engine Parts Ford
3	1	11	Bill Elliott	Budweiser Ford	24	34	52	Brad Teague	NAPA Ford
4	14	18	Dale Jarrett	Interstate Batteries Chevrolet	25	32	40	Bobby Hamilton	Kendall Pontiac
5	35	15	Lake Speed	Quality Care Ford	26	36	17	Darrell Waltrip	Western Auto Chevrolet
6	11	28	Ernie Irvan	Texaco Havoline Ford	27	27	27	Jimmy Spencer	McDonald's Ford
7	6	25	Ken Schrader	Kodiak Chevrolet	28	26	71	Dave Marcis	Style Motorsports Chevrolet
8	21	33	Harry Gant	Skoal Bandit Chevrolet	29	39	32	Dick Trickle	Active Motorsports Chevrolet
9	25	10	Ricky Rudd	Tide Ford	30	40	77	Greg Sacks	USAir Ford
10	20	16	Ted Musgrave	The Family Channel Ford	31	13	24	Jeff Gordon	DuPont Chevrolet
11	33	42	Kyle Petty	Mello Yello Pontiac	32	17	21	Morgan Shepherd	Citgo Ford
12	4	12	Chuck Bown	Lumberton Ford	33	8	2	Rusty Wallace	Miller Genuine Draft Ford
13	19	55	Jimmy Hensley	Petron Plus Ford	34	2	4	Sterling Marlin	Kodak Film Chevrolet
14	28	29	Steve Grissom	Diamond Ridge Chevrolet	35	24	5	Terry Labonte	Kellogg's Corn Flakes Chevrolet
15	30	30	Michael Waltrip	Pennzoil Pontiac	36	5	20	Brett Bodine	Quaker State Ford
16	12	98	Derrike Cope	Fingerhut Ford	37	10	1	Rick Mast	Skoal Classic Ford
17	15	23	Hut Stricklin	Smokin' Joe's Ford	38	18	14	John Andretti	Total Petroleum Chevrolet
18	23	90	Mike Wallace	Heilig-Meyers Ford	39	16	22	Bobby Labonte	Maxwell House Coffee Pontiac
19	29	41	Joe Nemechek	Meineke Mufflers Chevrolet	40	7	7	Geoff Bodine	Exide Batteries Ford
20	22	8	Jeff Burton	Raybestos Brakes Ford	41	37	43	Wally Dallenbach	STP Pontiac
21	38	31	Ward Burton	Hardee's Chevrolet					

FOOD CITY 500

BRISTOL INTERNATIONAL RACEWAY

APRIL 10, 1994

No driver in Larry Carrier's Bristol Raceway garage area was more anxious to get on with the program than Rusty Wallace. After back-to-back disappointments, Rusty and his Miller mates had fallen to 13th in the point standings and now trailed by a whopping 300 points. If the former champion had any hopes of adding a second NASCAR Winston Cup to his mantle in 1994, the Food City 500 was the place to take action.

(Top) Sterling Marlin takes the high road to work his way past Jeff Burton on his way to an eighth-place finish in the Kodak Chevrolet. (Right) Dale Earnhardt and wife Teresa celebrate his second consecutive victory.

Wallace, on the strength of nine consecutive first- or second-place finishes on short tracks, felt he had to make a move during the next three races on the schedule — Bristol, North Wilkesboro or Martinsville — if he was to have any hope of closing on the leaders.

Despite Dale Earnhardt's Darlington victory, Ernie Irvan still commanded the top rung of the point ladder, leading Earnhardt and Mark Martin (tied for second) by 81 points. Only 28 points separated Kenny Schrader, Ricky Rudd, Lake Speed and Morgan Shepherd in their battle for fourth place, but all were well out of sight of the leaders. Schrader was the closest, but he trailed by nearly 200 markers.

In another area of the garage, Jimmy Spencer was easing into the Mac Attack Ford after cracking his shoulder blade and writing off another Golden Arches machine in a North Wilkesboro test. And Dale Jarrett, after his sparkling fourth

Mark Martin started from the inside of the second row and his team kept him in contention until he was involved in a wreck with Jeff Gordon.

place at Darlington, had wrecked a pair of Interstate Batteries Chevrolets at a test session in North Wilkesboro.

Food City renewed its sponsorship of the April Bristol race for the next six years, and Carrier wasted no time beginning even more improvements for the steeply-banked Bristol bowl.

Goodyear brought a new tire to Bristol, and by the end of qualifying, nearly the entire field had eclipsed the track record. Leading the charge and continuing his recent string of outstanding qualifying performances was Chuck Bown, who became the third driver of the young season to win his first Winston Cup pole. Bown turned the fastest lap with Bobby Allison's Ford and nipped second-place qualifier Rusty Wallace by seven-thousandths of a second! Mark Martin guaranteed that Fords would occupy the first three positions, but Jeff Gordon broke the string by putting his DuPont Chevrolet in the fourth spot. Ted Musgrave qualified fifth, and Joe

Nemechek, the fastest driver on Hoosiers, would start from sixth position.

Irvan, Todd Bodine, Bobby Labonte and Morgan Shepherd completed the top 10. Earnhardt struggled to

Ricky Rudd was all smiles about the progress his young team had made early in the season. Despite a poor Bristol finish, Rudd was eighth in the standings after the race at Thunder Valley.

48

24th on the starting grid. Jeff Burton and Jarrett took provisionals to get into the field, and Darrell Waltrip was forced to exercise his former champion's provisional to start last. Among those who failed to qualify were: John Andretti, Jeremy Mayfield, Jimmy Hensley, Brad Teague and, once again, Loy Allen Jr.

Early in the race, it appeared that Rusty Wallace was a shoo-in for yet another short-track win. He and Jeff Gordon traded the lead in the first 140 laps. Rusty was at the point for more than 80 of the trips around the half-mile. But the Ford driver suffered tire problems just after mid-distance; he cut a tire while running third, and after blistering three more, he dropped to seventh place at the finish, six laps behind.

In the middle of the race, Geoff Bodine took just two tires from his back-side pit location and emerged at the front of the field. He led for 148 laps before making a green-flag stop, but that stop turned the tide toward a patient Earnhardt. Dale, Lake Speed and Schrader were the only cars yet to pit under green, so when the ninth yellow flew, those three had the advantage of being able to pit without losing a lap. They were the only cars on the lead lap, and that opened the door for Earnhardt to

Ernie Irvan's crew swarms over his Havoline Ford during the Food City 500, trying to make repairs to a sickly engine. Ernie was forced out after 167 laps.

Jeff Gordon had the dominant car in the first third of the race but later retired with wreck damage.

(Top) Chuck Bown bounces off the Bristol concrete while Joe Nemechek (41) and Todd Bodine (75) take different routes to avoid the wreck. (Left) Ernie Irvan came home a disappointing 33rd at Bristol.

post his second-straight victory with an easy 7.6-second lead over second-place Schrader. Speed was third in his best finish of the season. Geoff Bodine came home fourth, unable to make up his lap. He was, however, the highest-finishing Hoosier driver.

Michael Waltrip posted his first top five finish since 1992 by claiming fifth, but the Pennzoil Pontiac driver finished three laps behind after a flat tire caused him to limp to pit road. Bobby Labonte finished sixth in his Maxwell House Pontiac, two laps ahead of Wallace. Sterling Marlin, Bobby Hamilton and Dave Marcis completed the top 10.

Earnhardt's patient victory, coupled with engine problems for Irvan (33rd) and tire problems (along with wall damage) for Martin (21st), vaulted Earnhardt into the Winston Cup point lead after the sixth race of the year. Dale led by 40 points when the teams headed for North Wilkesboro.

Rusty Wallace battled tire problems and rode the Miller Genuine Draft Ford to a seventh-place finish.

Fin. Pos.	Str. Pos.	Car #	Driver	Team	Fin. Pos.	Str. Pos.	Car #	Driver	Team
1	24	3	Dale Earnhardt	GM Goodwrench Chevrolet	20	14	42	Kyle Petty	Mello Yello Pontiac
2	22	25	Ken Schrader	Kodiak Chevrolet	21	3	6	Mark Martin	Valvoline Ford
3	13	15	Lake Speed	Quality Care Ford	22	4	24	Jeff Gordon	DuPont Chevrolet
4	27	7	Geoff Bodine	Exide Batteries Ford	23	1	12	Chuck Bown	Masterbuilt Ford
5	23	30	Michael Waltrip	Pennzoil Pontiac	24	12	5	Terry Labonte	Kellogg's Corn Flakes Chevrolet
6	9	22	Bobby Labonte	Maxwell House Coffee Pontiac	25	21	31	Ward Burton	Hardee's Chevrolet
7	2	2	Rusty Wallace	Miller Genuine Draft Ford	26	8	75	Todd Bodine	Factory Stores of America Ford
8	18	4	Sterling Marlin	Kodak Film Chevrolet	27	17	98	Derrike Cope	Fingerhut Ford
9	34	40	Bobby Hamilton	Kendall Pontiac	28	25	90	Mike Wallace	Heilig-Meyers Ford
10	29	71	Dave Marcis	Style Motorsports Chevrolet	29	28	1	Rick Mast	Skoal Classic Ford
11	31	77	Greg Sacks	USAir Ford	30	15	11	Bill Elliott	Budweiser Ford
12	30	29	Steve Grissom	Diamond Ridge Chevrolet	31	35	8	Jeff Burton	Raybestos Brakes Ford
13	19	26	Brett Bodine	Quaker State Ford	32	11	10	Ricky Rudd	Tide Ford
14	26	23	Hut Stricklin	Smokin' Joe's Racing Ford	33	7	28	Ernie Irvan	Texaco Havoline Ford
15	37	17	Darrell Waltrip	Western Auto Chevrolet	34	32	32	Dick Trickle	Active Trucking Chevrolet
16	6	41	Joe Nemechek	Meineke Mufflers Chevrolet	35	16	27	Jimmy Spencer	McDonald's Ford
17	33	43	Wally Dallenbach	STP Pontiac	36	36	18	Dale Jarrett	Interstate Batteries Chevrolet
18	10	21	Morgan Shepherd	Citgo Ford	37	20	33	Harry Gant	Skoal Bandit Chevrolet
19	5	16	Ted Musgrave	The Family Channel Ford					

FIRST UNION 400

Following his second consecutive victory of the season at Bristol, Dale Earnhardt was whistling a happy tune while his Goodwrench team unloaded his Chevrolet at North Wilkesboro. Not only had Earnhardt taken over the point lead, but his two wins had helped Chevrolet pull even with Ford in the Manufacturer's Championship battle. Each marquee had three victories in the young season, and the score was tied at 45 points apiece.

(Top) Bobby Hamilton and Bill Elliott were forced to battle for mid-pack positions at the First Union 400.

(Right) Mark Martin looks over the competition at North Wilkesboro Speedway.

Rusty Wallace had a tight little grin on his face at times, as well. He had picked up 47 points at Bristol and had moved up from 13th to 10th in the standings. He now trailed by 253 but felt he had a real chance to take a swipe at the point lead in the next two events.

At Bristol the week before, Darrell Waltrip had jumped the Hoosier ship, deciding he would not be associated with a particular brand for the remainder of the year. The three-time champion was trying to get his team moving forward, and if it meant choosing between Goodyears or Hoosiers on a race-by-race basis, he was ready to play.

Throughout the first six races of the season, Fords had turned the fastest qualifying times. After the first session at Enoch Staley's five-eighths-mile roller coaster had been completed, the Blue Ovals' string was still intact. But this time, a different face was sitting on the seventh-straight pole for the Dearborn group.

tive at North Wilkesboro, claiming the fifth-fastest time. Greg Sacks, also on Hoosiers, sat alongside him. Sterling Marlin was the fastest non-Ford in the field, grabbing the inside of the fourth row with his Kodak Chevrolet. Jimmy Spencer proved there were some teeth in the Mac Attack with his spot alongside Marlin. Hendrick Motorsports teammates Ken Schrader and Terry Labonte made up the fifth row. But the surprise of first-round qualifying was young Jeremy Mayfield, who put the Sadler Racing Ford in the 11th-fastest spot.

Mark Martin would start 13th, and Dale Earnhardt made it into the first round 19th fastest. Jeff Burton and Bobby Labonte used provisionals to get into the field, but 10 cars and drivers went home to watch the race on ESPN. Those failing to qualify were: Jimmy Hensley, Steve Grissom, Joe Nemechek, Mike Wallace, Mike Skinner, Curtis Markham, Ward Burton, Freddy Query, Rich Bickle

Ernie Irvan bolted on the latest tire model from Goodyear and laid waste to Dale Earnhardt's track record, crunching the old mark by nearly 1.5 miles per hour. And Ernie was just the fastest of the fast. In all, 16 drivers surpassed the old mark!

Right alongside Irvan was former North Wilkesboro winner Brett Bodine. In a battle of motor oils, Bodine had plunked the green Quaker State Ford on the front row alongside Irvan's Havoline machine. Ted Musgrave and Bill Elliott made up the second row. Elliott had just missed the pole at Junior Johnson's "home" track.

Geoff Bodine showed that the Hoosiers were competi-

John Andretti found the concrete wall at North Wilkesboro and tore up Billy Hagan's Chevrolet.

Harry Gant posted an eighth-place finish at his "home" track in the spring North Wilkesboro event. He discovered that the inside lane was the right place to pass Bobby Labonte.

and Loy Allen.

From the outset, Ernie showed he had the right car for North Wilkesboro. Irvan led 320 of the first 328 laps and made a shambles of the competition. But under a yellow-flag pit stop on lap 328 -- the final caution of the day -- Ernie made a mistake and let his tire spin while a crew member was trying to tighten the lug nuts. The slip allowed Wallace, Kyle Petty and Labonte to beat Irvan from the pits, and since Ricky Rudd did not make a stop, Ernie was fifth in line for the restart. In addition, the tires on the Havoline Ford were mismatched (another consequence of the error), so what had appeared to be a dominant victory disintegrated into a third-place finish.

Rudd led for five laps, but Wallace's newer tires gave him enough of an edge to pass the Tide Ford. Behind him, Rusty could see Labonte mustering his strength to pass Rudd. After Terry moved the Kellogg's Chevrolet into second place on lap 360, Wallace knew he had a

fight on his hands. Terry, who had not visited a victory lane since 1989, had the juice today.

With 28 laps left, Labonte took the point. He moved under Rusty in the third turn and pulled away to a seven-second victory.

With his victory, Labonte helped Chevrolet take the Manufacturer's Championship point lead and moved himself to seventh in the point standings. Kyle Petty

Ernie Irvan's crew did everything they could to keep the Havoline Ford in contention, and it paid off with a "Big Picture" third place.

Jeff Burton takes to the inside with Dick Trickle and Bobby Labonte in tow.

finished fourth, his best outing of the year, just ahead of Earnhardt, who fought a slipping and sliding Chevrolet throughout the race. In the final 40 laps, he bested Ricky Rudd for fifth place.

Geoff Bodine and Harry Gant finished seventh and eighth, a lap down, and Rick Mast claimed a top 10 spot by finishing just behind Schrader.

By leading the most laps and finishing two spots ahead of Earnhardt, Irvan chopped 20 points from Dale's lead. The Havoline Ford driver was now just 20 points behind the leader.

A packed house watched Terry Labonte take the checkered flag.

Kyle Petty had it all together at North Wilkesboro; he finished fourth. Rusty Wallace used the outside line to pass Petty on his way to a second-place finish, four seconds behind Terry Labonte.

Fin. Pos.	Str. Pos.	Car #	Driver	Team	Fin. Pos.	Str. Pos.	Car #	Driver	Team
1	10	5	Terry Labonte	Kellogg's Corn Flakes Chevrolet	19	26	75	Todd Bodine	Factory Stores of America Ford
2	16	2	Rusty Wallace	Miller Genuine Draft Ford	20	14	23	Hut Stricklin	Smokin' Joe's Ford
3	1	28	Ernie Irvan	Texaco Havoline Ford	21	3	16	Ted Musgrave	The Family Channel Ford
4	28	42	Kyle Petty	Mello Yello Pontiac	22	15	21	Morgan Shepherd	Citgo Ford
5	19	3	Dale Earnhardt	GM Goodwrench Chevrolet	23	2	26	Brett Bodine	Quaker State Ford
6	25	10	Ricky Rudd	Tide Ford	24	34	32	Dick Trickle	Moinoke Mufflers Chevrolet
7	5	7	Geoff Bodine	Exide Batteries Ford	25	31	18	Dale Jarrett	Interstate Batteries Chevrolet
8	30	33	Harry Gant	Skoal Bandit Chevrolet	26	36	22	Bobby Labonte	Maxwell House Coffee Pontiac
9	9	25	Ken Schrader	Kodiak Chevrolet	27	22	98	Derrike Cope	Fingerhut Ford
10	17	1	Rick Mast	Skoal Classic Ford	28	33	17	Darrell Waltrip	Western Auto Chevrolet
11	18	30	Michael Waltrip	Pennzoil Pontiac	29	20	71	Dave Marcis	Terramite Chevrolet
12	29	15	Lake Speed	Quality Care Ford	30	11	95	Jeremy Mayfield	Shoney's Inns Ford
13	13	6	Mark Martin	Valvoline Ford	31	23	14	John Andretti	Financial World Chevrolet
14	24	40	Bobby Hamilton	Kendall Pontiac	32	8	27	Jimmy Spencer	McDonald's Ford
15	12	24	Jeff Gordon	DuPont Chevrolet	33	35	8	Jeff Burton	Raybestos Brakes Ford
16	27	43	Wally Dallenbach	STP Pontiac	34	6	77	Greg Sacks	USAir Ford
17	7	4	Sterling Marlin	Kodak Film Chevrolet	35	21	12	Chuck Bown	Allison Motorsports Ford
18	4	11	Bill Elliott	Budweiser Ford	36	32	78	Jay Hedgecock	Wilson-Inman Ford

HANES 500

After the races at Darlington two weeks earlier, Rusty Wallace had been 13th in the point standings and 300 points behind the leader. Since then, he had begun to make his move on the short tracks. Wallace was now 233 behind but had climbed to sixth place in the standings. He hadn't won at Bristol, but he had cruised to second at North Wilkesboro while watching Terry Labonte pull away to victory. Wallace now had arrived at the last of the races that comprise the first cycle of the tour around the bullrings. As the teams prepared for the Hanes 500 at Clay Earles' perfectly groomed half-mile, Wallace felt he had an outstanding chance to notch his second victory of the young season.

(Top) Usually, there's no place to go when someone gets out of shape at Martinsville. Here, Sterling Marlin becomes an obstacle to many contenders in the speedway's fourth turn. (Right) Rusty Wallace fought his way to a half-second victory over Ernie Irvan to claim the grandfather clock at Martinsville.

NASCAR announced that roof flaps would now be required on all tracks which were a mile or longer, with the exception of the road courses at Sears Point and Watkins Glen.

Meanwhile, pit road members were coming to terms with the losses of several members of the racing family. Bill Rexford, the 1950 NASCAR Grand National Champion, had died April 18 in Hemet, CA. Rexford was 23 (the youngest driver in NASCAR history to win the NASCAR Winston Cup title) when he defeated "Fireball" Roberts for the championship.

Several drivers also were reminiscing about former President Richard Nixon's recognition of stock car racing. Nixon had died the day of qualifying.

Miller
Genuine Draft
OAKLEY
NASCAR Winston Cup
Ford
BOSCH Spark Plugs
GOODYEAR
WINNER — APRIL 24 1994
HANES 500

Jeff Gordon struggled in his DuPont Chevrolet but finished to claim 33rd place at Martinsville.

The NASCAR family, although mourning the losses of its racing friends, was able to find solace in the pits as well. The cause for celebration was twofold. First, Bobby and Donna Labonte were uninjured in a crash-landing of Bobby's plane in Winston-Salem, NC, following the Atlanta race. Second, that same couple was now celebrating the birth of their first child, Robert Tyler, born April 18.

The teams had plenty on their minds, but it was back to business. The Unocal 76 bonus had not been claimed during the first seven races of the year and continued to accumulate. No driver had been able to win from the pole since Ernie Irvan turned the trick here at Martinsville last September. The bonus had ballooned to $98,800 — a hefty chunk of pocket money!

Darrell Waltrip's Western Auto Chevrolet sported Goodyears as the cars rolled to the line for qualifying. The three-time champion had made his decision to switch to the Eagles after running Goodyears at Bristol and Hoosiers at North Wilkesboro. He and Hoosier tire president Bob Newton had parted company.

When qualifying had been completed, yet another Ford driver sat on the pole, keeping the string intact. This time it was Rusty Wallace with the fastest lap. It was his first pole since Dover the previous September. Sterling Marlin was alongside him with another of Runt Pittman's "stump-puller" engines. Geoff Bodine upheld Hoosier's honor and plunked his Exide Ford third, and

Jimmy Spencer and the McDonald's Ford sat on the outside of the second row. Irvan was fifth, right beside Mark Martin, and Michael Waltrip and Dale Earnhardt made up the fourth row. Kyle Petty and Bill Elliott completed the top 10.

Once again, qualifying was as good a show as the race. Brett Bodine and Chuck Bown were forced to take provisional spots, and Curtis Markham again failed to qualify. Mike Wallace couldn't get Junie Donlavey's Ford in the field, and Jim Bown, Mike Skinner and Dave Marcis went home as well. Loy Allen missed the show and Wally Dallenbach was unable to qualify for Petty Enterprises. The biggest shock was Harry Gant's failure to make the field. It was the first time since the April '90 Bristol race (when his father died) that Harry was not in the field. His string ended at 118 races.

After the flag dropped Sunday afternoon, Rusty wasted no time establishing "Midnight Rider" as the dominant car in the field. He streaked to the lead, but then Geoff Bodine, who only took two tires when Rusty

Dale Jarrett lost his power steering and ended the day with a 21st-place finish.

took four on the second caution, moved the Exide Ford to the point. Wallace gave him the boot, however, in the fourth turn on lap 117. Rusty was able to motor to a four-second lead, but then he watched it disappear when the sixth yellow came out because of debris. No problem, the Miller driver decided. In the next 100 laps, he went back to the point to build an eight-second lead. Then Rusty was slapped with a penalty for speeding on pit

Rusty Wallace and Geoff Bodine exchanged the lead for the first half of the race, but Bodine later departed due to wreck damage. Rusty went on to win the race.

Earnhardt was getting a little frustrated. He had been penalized with a stop-and-go because his gas catch-can got caught on his car during a pit stop midway through the race and didn't fall off until three-quarters of a lap later. Later, Earnhardt spun and lost a lap after a collision with another car. The combination of Irvan's second place and Earnhardt's 11th had moved Ernie back into the point lead.

Behind the two black Fords, Mark Martin eased to third place ahead of a solid-running Darrell Waltrip, who was grinning after his fine finish. He was the only non-Ford driver in the top 10. Morgan Shepherd, in the Wood Brothers' Ford nicknamed "Old Ugly," was fifth at his team's home track, and Todd Bodine survived a spin to finish a career best sixth. Chuck Bown brought Bobby Allison's Ford home seventh ahead of Rick Mast and Bill Elliott, both a lap behind the pace. Ted Musgrave claimed the final top 10 position.

"Martinsville Maladies" had struck a variety of strong runners. Geoff Bodine,

road during the eighth caution. He was sent to the back of the line on the restart. By working hard on the track and taking advantage of his team's speed in the pits, Wallace was able to work his way back to second behind Irvan with 87 laps to go.

He dogged Ernie's every move but could not find a way past. The final caution flew for Dick Trickle's spin on lap 432, and the two black Fords headed for pit road. Both teams, working in adjacent bays, knew the stop could determine the race, and Wallace's team clicked the watch a tenth of a second faster. Rusty left pit road ahead of Ernie, and the two battled again. In the end, Wallace's Ford was too wide for Ernie to find a way past. The final margin was .43 of a second.

While Rusty was cashing the Unocal 76 bonus check,

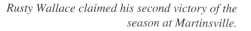

after leading early, cut a tire and spun. Dale Jarrett lost his power steering, Sterling Marlin and Jeff Gordon's cars failed to return after a collision, Jeff Burton lost his clutch and Ken Schrader suffered a leaking brake caliper.

Geoff Bodine had to settle for a 34th-place finish after a cut tire led to a meeting with the wall.

Fin. Pos.	Str. Pos.	Car #	Driver	Team	Fin. Pos.	Str. Pos.	Car #	Driver	Team
1	1	2	Rusty Wallace	Miller Genuine Draft Ford	19	22	22	Bobby Labonte	Maxwell House Coffee Pontiac
2	5	28	Ernie Irvan	Texaco Havoline Ford	20	26	23	Hut Stricklin	Smokin' Joe's Ford
3	6	6	Mark Martin	Valvoline Ford	21	20	18	Dale Jarrett	Interstate Batteries Chevrolet
4	16	17	Darrell Waltrip	Western Auto Chevrolet	22	29	41	Joe Nemechek	Meineke Mufflers Chevrolet
5	32	21	Morgan Shepherd	Citgo Ford	23	24	55	Jimmy Hensley	Petron Plus Ford
6	12	75	Todd Bodine	Factory Stores of America Ford	24	35	26	Brett Bodine	Quaker State Ford
7	36	12	Chuck Bown	ReLife Ford	25	31	78	Jay Hedgecock	Hauser Rental Ford
8	11	1	Rick Mast	Skoal Classic Ford	26	9	42	Kyle Petty	Mello Yello Pontiac
9	10	11	Bill Elliott	Budweiser Ford	27	2	4	Sterling Marlin	Kodak Film Chevrolet
10	28	16	Ted Musgrave	The Family Channel Ford	28	14	98	Derrike Cope	Fingerhut Ford
11	8	3	Dale Earnhardt	GM Goodwrench Chevrolet	29	18	77	Greg Sacks	USAir Ford
12	19	10	Ricky Rudd	Tide Ford	30	25	15	Lake Speed	Quality Care Ford
13	15	40	Bobby Hamilton	Kendall Pontiac	31	17	25	Ken Schrader	Kodiak Chevrolet
14	23	29	Steve Grissom	Diamond Ridge Chevrolet	32	34	32	Dick Trickle	Active Trucking Chevrolet
15	30	5	Terry Labonte	Kellogg's Corn Flakes Chevrolet	33	13	24	Jeff Gordon	DuPont Chevrolet
16	33	31	Ward Burton	Hardee's Chevrolet	34	3	7	Geoff Bodine	Exide Batteries Ford
17	7	30	Michael Waltrip	Pennzoil Pontiac	35	27	14	John Andretti	Financial World Chevrolet
18	4	27	Jimmy Spencer	McDonald's Ford	36	21	8	Jeff Burton	Raybestos Brakes Ford

63

WINSTON SELECT 500

TALLADEGA SUPERSPEEDWAY

MAY 1, 1994

Since departing from Darlington three races ago, Ernie Irvan and Dale Earnhardt had traded the series' point lead three times — Irvan had lost an 81-point lead only to regain it after Martinsville. The two had also battled in the first-quarter Driver of the Year balloting; Irvan just edged Earnhardt. Emerson Fittipaldi and Al Unser Jr. collected third and fourth place, respectively.

(Top) With his crew's help in the pits, Kyle Petty fought all day to finish 13th on the lead lap in the Winston Select 500. (Right) Dale Earnhardt's victory in the Winston Select 500, his third win of the season, qualified him for the 1994 Winston Select Million program.

So, with 20 points in hand, Irvan headed for Talladega and the Winston Select 500, the second event counting toward the Winston Select Million. Both programs were renamed this year after changes within R.J. Reynolds' marketing programs.

Mark Martin, who was tied for second in the point standings with Earnhardt after Darlington, now was third as the teams unloaded at the mammoth trioval in Alabama. Mark had lost 15 points in three races and could look over his shoulder and see Rusty Wallace. Wallace had made the move he needed — at least from his position in the point standings. He had traveled from 13th to fourth in three races and chopped 97 points off the lead. But now, he was at a track where he had never reaped much reward, and he trailed by 203. He needed a good finish this weekend.

The rest of the top 10 had remained stable throughout the three-race swing through the short tracks. There were some surprises: Kenny Schrader in fifth, Lake Speed sixth, Morgan Shepherd eighth, Terry Labonte ninth and Sterling Marlin dropping from eighth to 10th entering Talladega.

But the biggest surprise in the standings was seventh-place Rudd, who was startling the established teams with his rock-steady performances in his Tide Ford. Rudd had formed his own team over the winter, recruited out-of-work crew chief Billy Ingle, worked in leased space while his own shop was being constructed and turned in four

the first eight races (taking a provisional to get into the field at Rockingham), Allen had not seen action in his TriStar Ford since he sat on the pole at Atlanta in March.

Allen nearly made it three-for-three. On Hoosiers, he streaked around the track in a white, orange and blue blur and posted a lap at 193.193 mph. He immediately knew it wasn't enough, however, because minutes earlier, Irvan had laid one on the board at 193.298 mph.

Still, the front row would be made up of Fords, and Irvan's fast lap had stretched the string to nine for the Blue Ovals in '94. Todd Bodine, chalking up the third-fastest lap with his Factory Stores Ford, would start

At Talladega, Jimmy Spencer (27) and Sterling Marlin (4) make a USAir sandwich of Greg Sacks. Spencer finished fourth, Sacks sixth and Marlin eighth.

top 10 finishes in the first eight races.

There was a pair of drivers who couldn't wait to get started at Talladega. Sterling Marlin could put himself in the catbird seat in the Winston Select Million program with a victory. A win would eliminate everyone else and provide him with the two remaining opportunities to clinch the $1 million bonus.

The second was Loy Allen Jr. Allen knew his Hooters Ford would be fast, and after failing to qualify for six of

inside Earnhardt, the only non-Ford in the top six after the first round. Jimmy Spencer continued his good qualifying with the Mac Attack and claimed the fifth starting position alongside Greg Sacks. Schrader and Michael Waltrip made up the fourth row, and Chevrolet-driving Dale Jarrett and Marlin completed the top 10. Geoff Bodine, expected to make a bid for the pole, blew an engine while making his qualifying lap.

After both rounds had been completed, Bobby Labonte

Dale Earnhardt and Ernie Irvan line up to draft past Darrell Waltrip at the Winston Select 500.

and former Earnhardt crew chief Kirk Shelmerdine, driving Jimmy Means' Ford, became the provisional starters. Jim Sauter, Rich Bickle, Jimmy Horton, Ronnie Sanders, Delma Cowart and Ward Burton went home. Also making preparations to watch the Sunday race was Ritchie Petty, who failed to get Maurice Petty's Ford into the field.

Restrictor-plate races at Talladega have led to some of the most competitive racing in the sport over the last few years. Cars run two and three abreast, with drivers ducking and dodging throughout every lap, trying to find an advantage with one run-ningmate or another. It's white-knuckle stuff for the drivers, but it's pulse pounding, nail-biting, stand-on-your-seat racing for the hordes of fans who mob the huge track. Part of Talladega strategy is waiting until the closing laps to make your move and hoping you can avoid

Jimmy Spencer's "good luck" charms worked. The Mac Attack driver finished fourth.

trouble and be in the lead pack with a chance to win at the end.

This Sunday would be no different.

The lead swapped hands 20 times in the first 100 laps. Then, as Gordon tried to pass Sacks on lap 103, Sacks nudged Todd Bodine. When the smoke cleared, Rudd, Jeff Burton, Martin, Gordon, Chuck Bown and Allen had all been involved.

Just 10 laps later, Spencer and Terry Labonte tangled near the start/finish line. As a result of that collision, Rusty Wallace, Dick Trickle, Derrike Cope, Bown (again), Jeremy Mayfield, Jeff Purvis, Wally Dallenbach, Dale Jarrett, Harry Gant, Hut Stricklin and Jimmy Hensley lost their chances for a victory.

That left the race to a group that included Irvan, a hot-running Michael Waltrip, Marlin, Schrader, Spencer (with a little damage from the

John Andretti faces the media after the engine in his Chevrolet let go after 128 laps.

racing left, it was vintage Earnhardt.

In 10 laps, Earnhardt was third. One lap later, he was second. Ernie had tagged along, and he was right behind Earnhardt. Spencer was the leader, but it was merely a matter of time. Dale took the point on lap 184 and then withstood every challenge Spencer, Irvan, Schrader and Michael Waltrip could throw at him. Once they started racing amongst themselves, Earnhardt was home free for his seventh career NASCAR Winston Cup victory at Talladega. Irvan fought his way to second, Michael Waltrip third, Spencer fourth and Schrader fifth.

second wreck) and Earnhardt. With 17 laps left, Shelmerdine brought out the final yellow, setting up the dash to the finish. After changing tires, Earnhardt lined up 11th for the restart; Irvan lined up 17th, the final car on the lead lap. When the flag dropped with 21 laps of

Sacks survived to finish sixth. Speed followed Sacks, and Marlin came home eighth. Sterling now would have to battle Earnhardt in the Charlotte and Darlington races for the $1 million Winston bonus. Shepherd was ninth, and Steve Grissom finished tenth in his home state.

Ted Musgrave gives Rusty Wallace a boost as the two flash past Jimmy Hensley's Ford in the early going at Talladega. But Rusty had another tough day at 'Dega; he finished 33rd after being involved in a wreck.

At Talladega, pit work is crucial to keep cars in contention for the win. The slightest slip can mean the difference between running in the lead pack or finishing a lap down.

Fin. Pos.	Str. Pos.	Car #	Driver	Team	Fin. Pos.	Str. Pos.	Car #	Driver	Team
1	4	3	Dale Earnhardt	GM Goodwrench Chevrolet	22	41	22	Bobby Labonte	Maxwell House Coffee Pontiac
2	1	28	Ernie Irvan	Texaco Havoline Ford	23	13	33	Harry Gant	Skoal Bandit Chevrolet
3	8	30	Michael Waltrip	Pennzoil Pontiac	24	40	24	Jeff Gordon	DuPont Chevrolet
4	5	27	Jimmy Spencer	McDonald's Ford	25	33	10	Ricky Rudd	Tide Ford
5	7	25	Ken Schrader	Kodiak Chevrolet	26	42	52	Kirk Shelmerdine	Williams Racing Services Ford
6	6	77	Greg Sacks	USAir Ford	27	14	12	Chuck Bown	ReLife Ford
7	18	15	Lake Speed	Quality Care Ford	28	3	75	Todd Bodine	Factory Stores of America Ford
8	10	4	Sterling Marlin	Kodak Film Chevrolet	29	36	14	John Andretti	Financial World Chevrolet
9	12	21	Morgan Shepherd	Citgo Ford	30	29	55	Jimmy Hensley	Petron Plus Ford
10	11	29	Steve Grissom	Diamond Ridge Chevrolet	31	31	98	Derrike Cope	Fingerhut Ford
11	17	16	Ted Musgrave	The Family Channel Ford	32	21	5	Terry Labonte	Kellogg's Corn Flakes Chevrolet
12	39	40	Bobby Hamilton	Kendall Pontiac	33	20	2	Rusty Wallace	Miller Genuine Draft Ford
13	27	42	Kyle Petty	Mello Yello Pontiac	34	35	43	Wally Dallenbach	STP Pontiac
14	16	17	Darrell Waltrip	Western Auto Chevrolet	35	32	51	Jeff Purvis	Country Time Chevrolet
15	19	90	Mike Wallace	Heilig-Meyers Ford	36	38	32	Dick Trickle	ATS Wood Recycling Chevrolet
16	22	71	Dave Marcis	STG Chevrolet	37	24	95	Jeremy Mayfield	Shoney's Inn Ford
17	28	26	Brett Bodine	Quaker State Ford	38	15	6	Mark Martin	Valvoline Ford
18	26	23	Hut Stricklin	Smokin' Joe's Ford	39	34	8	Jeff Burton	Raybestos Brakes Ford
19	30	11	Bill Elliott	Budweiser Ford	40	2	19	Loy Allen	Hooters Ford
20	25	1	Rick Mast	Skoal Classic Ford	41	23	7	Geoff Bodine	Exide Batteries Ford
21	9	18	Dale Jarrett	Interstate Batteries Chevrolet	42	37	41	Joe Nemechek	Meineke Mufflers Chevrolet

SAVE MART SUPERMARKETS 300

For the sixth time, the NASCAR Winston Cup tour headed for northern California's Bay Area, but it was the first time a native Californian would return to California as the series point leader.

Two years ago, Ernie Irvan had delighted his home-state fans by emerging as the winner at the conclusion of the Sears Point race. He finished second last year, less than a half-second behind Geoff Bodine. Both of those finishes at the serpentine track nestled in the California wine country had been Kodak Moments for Irvan.

But for Ernie, this trip resembled the return of a conquering hero. Through all the promotional appearances (part of the territory when one is at the top of the point ladder), the Havoline Ford driver insisted that there were two reasons for his success in the first nine races of the season. The first was the hard work and dedication of his crew, who, week after week, had given him machinery and motors capable of running at the front of the pack.

The second was the wizardry and coaching of crew chief Larry McReynolds.

Irvan explained that McReynolds and car owner Robert Yates reminded him daily ("Sometimes, it seems like hourly!") that the goal of this 10-month odyssey is the Winston Cup championship, not just single event titles. "Larry, Robert and all of us, including myself, want to win races. If that's what we can do on a given Sunday, then that's what we'll do. But if all we can do is get a second or a fifth or a tenth — if that's the best we can do that day — then that's what our goal is. We want to be consistent ... get every position we can without causing a problem in finishing. That

(Top) The Fords of Ernie Irvan and Mark Martin lead the pack from the starting line at Sears Point. (Right) Throughout the day, Robert Yates' crew kept Ernie Irvan in contention for the win with great pit work.

70

Derrike Cope didn't enjoy his trip to the California wine country.

Rusty Wallace also found himself with problems. Talladega had been unkind to him again, and Wallace was back to seventh in the points — a whopping 319 behind the leader.

When Geoff Bodine, last year's winner, lost a cylinder at the start of his qualifying lap, and Lake Speed, driving the car Bodine won in last year, was able to use third gear only, Irvan took advantage of the situation. He put the torch to the Havoline Ford and won his third pole of the season, keeping Ford's string of poles alive. Ernie's lap moved fellow Ford driver Mark Martin back to second place, but Mark was still pleased. He had wrecked in practice, so his Valvoline team had to rebuild the front end. His qualifying lap was the first he turned after the repairs and was also his first

consistency is what will win the championship, not winning one week and finishing last the next because we did something stupid. They keep reminding me of the big picture," Ernie said.

Dale Earnhardt's victory at Talladega put Chevrolet in the lead in the Manufacturer's Championship, and the driver of the black Chevrolet now had a series-leading three victories in the first nine races.

Kenny Schrader's crew prepares for his arrival; they realize that every pit stop is crucial. The crew helped Schrader to a ninth-place finish.

Any way it works! Ted Musgrave clips the curb at the top of the hill at Sears Point.

on new tires. He called his lap "on the conservative side of wildness," and said he was just happy to be on the front row.

Ricky Rudd, always a contender on a road course, had the third-fastest lap, moving Earnhardt down to fourth at the end of the first day. Terry Labonte, showing he had not lost his road-racing skills, claimed fifth ahead of Jeff Gordon. Wally Dallenbach, who cut his teeth on this race track and nearly won while driving for Jack Roush, placed the Petty Enterprises Pontiac a sparkling seventh, inside Ken Schrader and ahead of Michael Waltrip and Kyle Petty. Butch Gilliland was the fastest NASCAR Winston West competitor field, starting 15th, and Rick Carelli made a Cup start, qualifying 36th.

Greg Sacks and Chuck Bown took the provisional spots, and Gary Collins claimed the NASCAR Winston West provisional. Those

At Sears Point, Winston West competitor Mike Chase found that the tire wall was a difficult place to drive away from.

who made the cross-country trip in vain were NASCAR Winston Cup regulars Dick Trickle, Jimmy Hensley and Loy Allen. In addition, Scott Gaylord just missed getting Jimmy Means' Ford into the field.

While the last of the huge crowd poured through the gates, Irvan blasted away at the drop of the green flag and was never passed on the track. He lost the lead briefly on pit road when Dale Earnhardt's crew put him out first, and Irvan gave up the point twice during green-flag stops. But each time, he was immediately back to the front, dominating the race. Ernie put the Ford in cruise control, and when Geoff Bodine made a run in the waning laps, Ernie merely stepped up his pace to maintain his near 10-second lead. It was a flawless performance for Yates, McReynolds, the crew and the Californian, who had won the third road-course trophy of his career.

Bodine, who came from 26th

place at the start, was pleased with his second-place finish on Hoosier tires. Despite his praise for the Purple H tires, the score still remained Goodyear 10-Hoosier 0 after the first third of the season.

Earnhardt refused to let Irvan out of his sight. He turned in a workmanlike performance and walked away from Sears Point with third place. He had lost 15 points to Irvan and now trailed by 40, but he was right where he wanted to be with eight top 10 finishes in the first 10 races.

Dallenbach delighted car owner Richard Petty with a fourth-place finish, and Wallace came home fifth after running as high as second with a new road-racing chassis from Penske South. Musgrave and Shepherd finished sixth and seventh, ahead of Martin, Schrader and Harry Gant, who was beginning his last trip around the race tracks in this final season of competition.

When the snoozes hit, any place will do.

74

Rookie of the Year contender Jeff Burton came home 15th in the Raybestos Ford.

Fin. Pos.	Str. Pos.	Car #	Driver	Team	Fin. Pos.	Str. Pos.	Car #	Driver	Team
1	1	28	Ernie Irvan	Texaco Havoline Ford	23	28	90	Mike Wallace	Heilig-Meyers Ford
2	26	7	Geoff Bodine	Exide Batteries Ford	24	42	77	Greg Sacks	USAir Ford
3	4	3	Dale Earnhardt	GM Goodwrench Chevrolet	25	39	71	Dave Marcis	Health Management Chevrolet
4	7	43	Wally Dallenbach	STP Pontiac	26	25	27	Jimmy Spencer	McDonald's Ford
5	12	2	Rusty Wallace	Miller Genuine Draft Ford	27	14	36	Butch Gilliland	Gilliland Racing Chevrolet
6	15	16	Ted Musgrave	The Family Channel Ford	28	5	5	Terry Labonte	Kellogg's Corn Flakes Chevrolet
7	19	21	Morgan Shepherd	Citgo Ford	29	13	4	Sterling Marlin	Kodak Film Chevrolet
8	2	6	Mark Martin	Valvoline Ford	30	11	11	Bill Elliott	Budweiser Ford
9	8	25	Ken Schrader	Kodiak Chevrolet	31	35	50	Mike Chase	Star Race Computers Chevrolet
10	16	33	Harry Gant	Skoal Bandit Chevrolet	32	29	15	Lake Speed	Quality Care Ford
11	10	42	Kyle Petty	Mello Yello Pontiac	33	30	40	Bobby Hamilton	Kendall Pontiac
12	20	18	Dale Jarrett	Interstate Batteries Chevrolet	34	24	1	Rick Mast	Skoal Classic Ford
13	23	26	Brett Bodine	Quaker State Ford	35	40	29	Steve Grissom	Diamond Ridge Chevrolet
14	3	10	Ricky Rudd	Tide Ford	36	27	31	Ward Burton	Hardee's Chevrolet
15	21	8	Jeff Burton	Raybestos Brakes Ford	37	6	24	Jeff Gordon	DuPont Chevrolet
16	9	30	Michael Waltrip	Pennzoil Pontiac	38	31	75	Todd Bodine	Factory Stores of America Ford
17	22	22	Bobby Labonte	Maxwell House Coffee Pontiac	39	18	76	Ron Hornaday	Spears Mfg. Chevrolet
18	33	17	Darrell Waltrip	Western Auto Chevrolet	40	43	20	Gary Collins	Veneble Racing Ford
19	38	14	John Andretti	Financial World Chevrolet	41	36	61	Rick Carelli	Total Petroleum Chevrolet
20	37	23	Hut Stricklin	Smokin' Joe's Ford	42	34	9	John Krebs	Channelock Chevrolet
21	41	12	Chuck Bown	ReLife Ford	43	17	98	Derrike Cope	Fingerhut Ford
22	32	41	Joe Nemechek	Meineke Mufflers Chevrolet					

WINSTON SELECT

MAY 21, 1994

It's hard to believe that this all-star race is 10 years old! And for all nine previous runnings of the race, fans remember – and can recount for you second-by-second – what happened in each of NASCAR's version of the all-star game. Quick:

'85 – Darrell Waltrip blows engine at the start/finish line after catching Gant.

'86 – Redhead makes mincemeat of everyone at Atlanta.

'87 – Bodine, the Redhead and Earnhardt. Pass in the Grass. Enough said.

'88 – Labonte makes up lap, runs away to give Junior second win.

'89 – No yawns here. Rusty, Darrell. Spin and Win.

'90 – Goodwrench runaway. Dale's second trophy.

'91 – Behind the woodshed with Davey. Havoline Holiday.

'92 – Final Lap Fireworks under the lights. Davey and Kyle in a shower of sparks. Robert Yates accepts trophy!

'93 – Dale jumps restart flag with two to go. Restart. Big E blasts past Mark in third turn of final lap. Third trophy for Earnhardt.

After the past two years' finishes, no one knew what to expect this May. Would the Winston Select – renamed by sponsor R.J. Reynolds for a new Winston brand – be another thriller or would it turn out to be a slow one?

(Top) Darrell Waltrip powers the Western Auto Chevrolet underneath Morgan Shepherd's Citgo Ford on his way to a fourth-place finish. (Right) Geoff and Kathy Bodine were all smiles after their first victory as co-owners of the team.

Ward Burton and Joe Nemechek (41) transferred into the final starting spots in the Winston Select by virtue of their performances in the Open.

Qualifying for the Select lineup again consisted of three laps on the track, including a two-tire pit stop, which offered every crew the chance to make a difference in its driver's starting position. Total time determined the starting position, not miles per hour turned by the driver.

On the basis of pit road times produced during the first third of the season, Rusty Wallace and his Miller team were the favorites. When qualifying had been completed, Rusty's crew had lived up to its billing. All the Miller crew did was give Rusty two tires in a record 10.13 seconds – six-tenths of a second faster than the old mark set last year by Tony Glover and his Kodak mighty-mites. Wallace also did his part, lighting up both ends of pit road to gain the pole and its $50,000 prize.

Ricky Rudd's team surprised everyone on pit road with the next-fastest stop, cranking a 10.16. But Rudd was penalized a second for a loose lug nut and wound up starting sixth. Ernie Irvan earned the outside of the front row, ahead of Dale Jarrett and Geoff Bodine. Terry Labonte was inside Rudd, and Bill Elliott and Morgan Shepherd occupied the fourth row. Kyle Petty and Lake Speed were ninth and 10th. Dale Earnhardt was 11th following a slow, 14-second stop from the "Flying Aces."

The Yates Racing crew provides service between the first and second segments of the Winston Select. The Texaco Havoline Ford was the class of the field until Ernie tried (unsuccessfully) to repeat history with another Pass in the Grass.

The Winston Select weekend is a time to run wide open and have a good time since no points are on the line. Here, Junior Johnson encourages his driver to be less conservative.

Six positions were still available in the main event, and the Open offered 36 competitors a chance to get into "The Show." On lap 30, however, 11 drivers' chances to compete in the Select were eliminated. Dave Marcis was leading after a restart when Ward Burton drew alongside to try to pass him. The two touched, and everyone started scrambling behind them. Among those involved were: Ken Bouchard, Chuck Bown, Harry Gant, Michael Waltrip, John Andretti, Todd Bodine, Brett Bodine, Wally Dallenbach, Rich Bickle and Loy Allen. Dallenbach and Brett Bodine were able to continue.

That left the Open to Jeff Gordon, and he picked his way to a 3.5-second victory over Greg Sacks, Kenny Schrader and Jeff Burton. Ward Burton made it through the accident and finished fifth, and Joe Nemechek took the sixth and final transfer spot.

The Open fireworks only whetted the huge crowd's appetite for the Winston Select.

In the main event, just before the halfway point of the first segment, Marlin and Geoff Bodine touched. Bodine slid down the frontstretch and looped his Exide Ford. From that point on, Irvan displayed the strength of his Ford and streaked to the $50,000 untouched. The fans had voted nine-to-one to invert the start of the second half, so Bodine watched anxiously as his team made hasty repairs. Terry Labonte's Kellogg's Chevrolet suffered transmission problems, and Terry was unable to start the second segment.

Irvan and Marlin started on the last row, but Ernie lost no time flying through the field. After 11 laps, he was up to eighth. A caution flew after Ward Burton tried to insert his Hardee's Ford between Earnhardt and Irvan. Ward went sliding, and Mark Martin barely missed him. But that was only the beginning.

On the 50th lap, Earnhardt bumped Wallace, eliminating either from winning the all-star event again. Gordon was a casualty as well. Four laps later, Greg Sacks and Martin got together, and both smacked the wall between one and two. Had enough? Not yet!

On the final lap of the second segment, Irvan temporarily abandoned the "Big Picture" theory. Irvan must have been thinking about artist Garry Hill's painting, the famed "Pass In The Grass," between Earnhardt and Elliott in 1987. Ernie dove under leader Bodine, put his left-side tires in the grass in a desperate attempt to beat Bodine to the flag at the end of the second segment and then lost control.

Bodine led entering the final ten laps while the field self-destructed all around him. But Schrader had something for the Hoosier-shod Ford driver, and Kenny wasted no time showing Bodine the tail of the Kodiak Chevrolet. Marlin followed Schrader through, and suddenly Bodine was third. But Bodine finally got

hooked up, and with just three laps remaining, Bodine dove to the inside of the third turn and pulled clear exiting the fourth while the two Chevrolets raced side by side. Geoff eased away and watched in his mirror as Marlin edged Schrader in a photo finish for second. Darrell Waltrip was fourth, ahead of Rudd and Jeff Burton.

It was Bodine's first victory since he had bought Alan Kulwicki's team. Alan had ordered the victorious car after he lost a car in Atlanta in March 1993, and the car was to have competed in the 1993 running of The Winston and the Coca-Cola 600. Work on the car, however, was not completed until last fall, so Bodine drove it in the Mello Yello 500.

After taking the checkered flag, Geoff stopped and turned the Exide Ford around. He made a slow "Polish Victory Lap," the first – and he said later, only – time he would do so, to honor Alan. "I felt like Alan was in the car with me during those last few laps," Bodine said after the race. "A little over a year ago, this team was Alan's. We did the lap in honor of him, and we dedicate this victory to him."

Derrike Cope (98) and Ted Musgrave battled hard in the Open but were unable to transfer into the main event.

Some of the cars were decorated with reflective decals, which added to the glitter of NASCAR's all-star event.

WINSTON SELECT - FINAL RESULTS

Fin. Pos.	Str. Pos.	Car #	Driver	Team	Fin. Pos.	Str. Pos.	Car #	Driver	Team
1	4	7	Geoff Bodine	Exide Batteries Ford	11	9	42	Kyle Petty	Mello Yello Pontiac
2	14	4	Sterling Marlin	Kodak Chevrolet	12	7	11	Bill Elliott	Budweiser Ford
3	17	25	Ken Schrader	Kodiak Chevrolet	13	10	15	Lake Speed	Quality Care Ford
4	13	17	Darrell Waltrip	Western Auto Chevrolet	14	15	24	Jeff Gordon	DuPont Chevrolet
5	6	10	Ricky Rudd	Tide Ford	15	3	28	Ernie Irvan	Havoline Ford
6	18	8	Jeff Burton	Raybestos Ford	16	12	6	Mark Martin	Valvoline Ford
7	3	18	Dale Jarrett	Interstate Batteries Chevrolet	17	16	77	Greg Sacks	USAir Ford
8	8	21	Morgan Shepherd	Citgo Ford	18	11	3	Dale Earnhardt	GM Goodwrench Chevrolet
9	19	31	Ward Burton	Hardee's Chevrolet	19	1	2	Rusty Wallace	Miller Genuine Draft Ford
10	20	41	Joe Nemechek	Meineke Mufflers Chevrolet	20	5	5	Terry Labonte	Kellogg's Corn Flakes Chevrolet

COCA-COLA 600

CHARLOTTE MOTOR SPEEDWAY

MAY 29, 1994

Geoff Bodine's celebration of his victory in the Winston Select had barely ended before it was "back to business" for the NASCAR Winston Cup teams. The Coca-Cola 600 loomed large on the horizon, and this race, the longest of the year, paid points. No more "special" events for the season!

(Top) Geoff Bodine's Exide Ford was the dominant car in the early going of the Coca-Cola 600. (Right) Jeff Gordon makes a move on Michael Waltrip. Gordon drove the DuPont Refinishes Chevrolet to the pole position and victory lane.

Bodine's victory on Hoosiers had finally put the tire company in victory lane. Throughout the Winston Select weekend, many felt that the winner would be Hoosier-clad. The tires had been blisteringly fast in qualifying, and if teams — as Bodine's had — got the chassis package right, most believed that the tires would last until the end.

No one knew what to expect from the Hoosiers for the 600, however. The race would begin in the heat of the day and finish under the lights, offering competitors a changing track surface throughout the 400-lap race.

Joe Nemechek had destroyed Alan Kulwicki's old track record by nearly 2.5 mph while qualifying (on Hoosiers) for the Winston Select Open. Many expected more of the same when it came time for 600 qualifying. And when qualifying had been completed, a Chevrolet finally sat on a point-race pole this season, but it wasn't Nemechek on the sticky Hoosiers.

rather than use a backup, the team toiled throughout the hours between the end of the Winston Select and the opening of practice to re-body the Ford. When he ran in qualifying, the right side of the car was still peanut-butter colored bondo. The team finally put the white, red and blue paint on the car at the track after qualifying had been completed! It was a similar story for several teams.

In all, 13 of the cars in the field for the 600 would be on Hoosiers. Bobby Hillin, Jimmy Hensley and Jim Sauter failed to make the field. Also missing the field, despite using a Richard Childress-owned Chevrolet painted in Olive Garden colors, was Dave Marcis. Marcis had made 26 consecutive 600 starts, but his string came to an end in 1994. Kyle Petty, unable to figure out the aero characteristics of the new Pontiac extensions, took one provisional while Ted Musgrave claimed the second. Bill Elliott struggled and was forced to take the former champion's provisional, starting last in the field.

This year's Coca-Cola 600 produced a page of history and more than its share of drama. Andretti, who finished 10th in the Indy 500 earlier in the day, commandeered both jets and helicopters to transport him to Charlotte, where he landed near the start/finish line just in time to buckle in for the 600. He became the first driver ever to compete in both races the same day. Because he had missed the driver's

Jeff Gordon, driving a car rebuilt after his wreck in the Winston Select, had run horribly in the first round of qualifying and finished fourth from last. But with the help of a rain delay that cooled the track, he was able to slap the DuPont Chevrolet on the pole with a "gotcha" lap of 181.439 mph. Nemechek settled for the outside of the front row, more than a mile per hour slower. Geoff Bodine continued his chassis mastery and took third for the start alongside Kenny Schrader. Brett Bodine and Greg Sacks made up the third row, and Rick Mast and Ward Burton qualified ahead of John Andretti and Terry Labonte. Point leader Ernie Irvan was 14th in a backup car, Rusty was 21st, and Dale Earnhardt placed 24th. Jeremy Mayfield was the new driver for T.W. Taylor at Charlotte; he had moved from the Sadler team to replace Curtis Markham.

Many of the drivers were using their "second choice" cars after the damage of the previous weekend. Mark Martin, however, liked his Valvoline Ford so much that,

Dale Earnhardt and crew chief Andy Petree studied all the angles in an effort to notch a Charlotte win but finished ninth instead.

meeting, he was forced to start at the rear of the 600 field. On the 90th lap, his efforts ended with a spin. Repairs were made, but the engine failed after 220 laps.

Rusty and his Miller mates, trailing Irvan by 349 points, knew they had to make something happen soon, and Wallace was determined it would be at Charlotte. As the first half of the race ground away, Wallace finally surfaced at the front on lap 164 and was dominant for the remainder of the race, leading the most laps. He scrapped with Earnhardt, who had fallen a lap down, and then battled with Irvan and Geoff Bodine, who had his Exide Ford at the front of the field again. But just when it looked like Wallace was ready to win, the race

Ricky Rudd heads up the pack at Charlotte. He would finish the day sixth after qualifying 13th.

changed dramatically.

The final 77 laps of the race were run under green, and one by one, drivers on the lead lap pitted for a final fuel stop. Gordon hung tough until all the other leaders pitted. His crew chief, Ray Evernham, took a look around and rolled the dice. Every other driver had taken four tires during his stop. A two-tire stop would be quicker, but would Gordon be able to combat the others, who had four fresh Goodyears or Hoosiers, with only two fresh tires?

Gordon took right-sides and emerged in second place behind Ricky Rudd, who was trying to steal the win by going all the way

Kenny Schrader and Greg Sacks battle at Charlotte; Schrader finished 10 laps ahead of the USAir Ford.

on his fuel. But Rudd hit pit road with nine laps to go, and Gordon retook the lead. Rusty put the hammer down in hopes of catching Gordon, but he had nothing left for the 23-year-old. Blinking away his tears of joy, Gordon took the checkered flag and headed for victory lane.

Met there by Brooke Sealey, his fiancee, the realization of what he had done began to set in. His first career victory had come in one of the most grueling, difficult races of the year.

Wallace finished second; Geoff Bodine third. Dale Jarrett survived for a solid fourth place. Irvan kept pace with the challengers, taking home a hard-fought fifth, ahead of Rudd and Harry Gant, who completed his final 600 one lap in arrears. Todd Bodine finished eighth and Earnhardt ninth. Earnhardt and 10th-place finisher Michael Waltrip both finished three laps down.

After two weeks at Charlotte, the teams were ready to move on. Dover's "Monster Mile" was next on the schedule.

Wreck damage sent Mark Martin to pit road in search of assistance. Mark finished 32nd after a long day.

A gamble by crew chief Ray Evernham (he gave Jeff Gordon only two tires during the final pit stop) enabled the young driver to win his first NASCAR Winston Cup race.

Joe Nemechek found it impossible to handle the muscle of Jeff Gordon and Mark Martin in the Coca-Cola 600.

Fin. Pos.	Str. Pos.	Car #	Driver	Team	Fin. Pos.	Str. Pos.	Car #	Driver	Team
1	1	24	Jeff Gordon	DuPont Chevrolet	23	35	90	Mike Wallace	Heilig-Meyers Ford
2	21	2	Rusty Wallace	Miller Genuine Draft Ford	24	4	25	Ken Schrader	Kodiak Chevrolet
3	3	7	Geoff Bodine	Exide Batteries Ford	25	12	43	Wally Dallenbach	STP Pontiac
4	16	18	Dale Jarrett	Interstate Batteries Chevrolet	26	41	42	Kyle Petty	Mello Yello Pontiac
5	14	28	Ernie Irvan	Texaco Havoline Ford	27	6	77	Greg Sacks	USAir Ford
6	13	10	Ricky Rudd	Tide Ford	28	17	21	Morgan Shepherd	Citgo Ford
7	18	33	Harry Gant	Skoal Bandit Chevrolet	29	15	8	Jeff Burton	Raybestos Brakes Ford
8	31	75	Todd Bodine	Factory Stores of America Ford	30	29	17	Darrell Waltrip	Western Auto Chevrolet
9	24	3	Dale Earnhardt	GM Goodwrench Chevrolet	31	7	1	Rick Mast	Skoal Classic Ford
10	30	30	Michael Waltrip	Pennzoil Pontiac	32	11	6	Mark Martin	Valvoline Ford
11	37	19	Loy Allen	Hooters Ford	33	2	41	Joe Nemechek	Meineke Mufflers Chevrolet
12	40	23	Hut Stricklin	Smokin' Joe's Ford	34	26	9	Rich Bickle	Orkin Ford
13	20	12	Chuck Bown	Bobby Allison Motorsports Ford	35	10	5	Terry Labonte	Kellogg's Corn Flakes Chevrolet
14	39	15	Lake Speed	Quality Care Ford	36	9	14	John Andretti	Bryant Heating/Cooling Chevrolet
15	32	4	Sterling Marlin	Kodak Film Chevrolet	37	8	31	Ward Burton	Hardee's Chevrolet
16	42	16	Ted Musgrave	The Family Channel Ford	38	36	32	Dick Trickle	Active Racing Chevrolet
17	23	40	Bobby Hamilton	Kendall Pontiac	39	28	29	Steve Grissom	Diamond Ridge Chevrolet
18	22	98	Derrike Cope	Fingerhut Ford	40	25	22	Bobby Labonte	Maxwell House Coffee Pontiac
19	33	27	Jimmy Spencer	McDonald's Ford	41	38	52	Brad Teague	Means Racing Ford
20	27	20	Randy LaJoie	Fina Lube Ford	42	5	26	Brett Bodine	Quaker State Ford
21	19	02	Jeremy Mayfield	Children's Miracle Network Ford	43	34	47	Billy Standridge	Standridge Auto Parts Ford
22	43	11	Bill Elliott	Budweiser Ford					

BUDWEISER 500

DOVER DOWNS
INTERNATIONAL SPEEDWAY

JUNE 5, 1994

The fortnight at Charlotte was in the history books. Teams were now unloading at Denis McGlynn's "Monster Mile" with a variety of emotions.

Ernie Irvan, with crew chief Larry McReynolds and car owner Robert Yates constantly reminding him about the Big Picture, used his fifth place at Charlotte to pad his point lead. He was now 62 points ahead of Dale Earnhardt after the first third of the season.

Jeff Gordon couldn't have won at a better time. He came to Dover as the conquering hero, and his sponsor, located just an hour north of Dover Downs, treated him like royalty. Nothing like appearing in your sponsor's backyard with a trophy from the previous race to keep those folks smiling!

On the other hand, Mark Martin's Charlotte fortunes had been disastrous. He was 354 points behind. At the season's end, Mark might look to Charlotte to explain what went wrong with his championship bid.

Rusty Wallace had had the dominant car in the 600, but he still lost. The good news was that his second place moved him from sixth to third in the point standings. The bad news was he remained 329 behind the leader. Not yet time to panic, Rusty reassured everyone who asked, but a grim determination underscored every move by his team.

Michael Waltrip had moved to 10th in the standings with his fourth top 10 finish of the season. He was on the lead

(Top) Neither Terry Labonte nor Ted Musgrave had a great showing at Dover. (Right) Barry Henzi, jackman for Joe Nemechek's team, heads for the left side of the car after the right-side work had been completed.

Derrike Cope emerged as the winner of this battle with Morgan Shepherd in the Budweiser 500 at Dover.

lap in only one of those finishes, but the Pennzoil Pontiac had become the standard-bearer for the General Motors brand.

That trend hadn't been lost on Mello Yello Pontiac owner Felix Sabates. His driver, Kyle Petty, had to take a provisional at the event which was sponsored by Mello Yello's parent company, Coca-Cola. Kyle had recorded only two top-five finishes for the season by the end of the Coke 600. Monday morning, general manager Robin Pemberton was released from the team along with his two brothers, Ryan, the team's tire specialist and mechanic, and Roman, a tire-changer on weekends and mechanic at the shop during the week.

Gordon's victory had demonstrated that Goodyear had brought the right tire to Charlotte. But every event was different, and

"Ricky, what you have to do is get tough with your car owner when it comes to negotiating your salary for next season." Rudd, despite Darrell Waltrip's advice, appears to know what his car owner will say to his increased salary demands!

Workers come to the aid of Brett Bodine after his Ford cracked the concrete wall.

as the teams prepared for qualifying, few knew which tire would provide an advantage at Dover.

And at the end of the first round, there was still no consensus of opinion. Irvan had streaked to his fourth pole of the season on Goodyears, but less than a tenth of a second behind was Geoff Bodine — on Hoosiers. Joe Nemechek had claimed the inside of the second row, but Bobby Labonte, with his best qualifying effort of the season, was fourth-fastest. Bill Elliott, still smarting from having to take the former champion's provisional spot (last in the field) at Charlotte, qualified fifth, just inside Wallace. Ted Musgrave and Bobby

Hamilton claimed the fourth row, and Morgan Shepherd and Jimmy Hensley grabbed the final spots in the top 10. Earnhardt qualified 14th.

Others who had been expected to challenge had problems. Michael Waltrip crashed in the final practice session and didn't run first-round qualifying. An oil fire broke out in Martin's Ford while it was sitting on pit road prior to qualifying. Jimmy Spencer spun on his qualifying lap, and Gordon scuffed the wall during his lap. After both rounds had

After leading early in the race, Geoff Bodine, hoping for a good finish in his Exide Ford, instead ended his day in a confrontation with the Dover wall.

Yates Racing jackman Jeff Clark rolls a used tire toward crew chief Larry McReynolds during a pit stop at Dover.

by NASCAR, Ford, Dover Downs, R.J. Reynolds and his former drivers with a variety of plaques and gifts.

Dover has always been one of the most difficult races on the circuit. The track is a mile in length, which equals 500 laps for competitors before the end of the afternoon, and has a history of wearing out man and machine. This event on the first Sunday in June would be no different.

The race turned into a furious battle between Irvan and Wallace, who took turns leading until the final caution came out (when Bobby Labonte hit the fourth-turn wall after being tagged by John Andretti) with just eight laps remaining. Wallace's 1.25-second lead was erased, and when the field took the green flag for the final sprint with just five laps remaining, Irvan was given one last chance to catch Wallace. But Rusty was not about to let this one get away; he eased to a three-car-length victory over the Havoline Ford. Ken Schrader finished third, ahead of Martin and Gordon, who survived overheating problems with his Chevrolet.

Darrell and Michael Waltrip had their personal battle for sixth, a lap in arrears. In the end, Darrell showed his younger brother the way home. Sterling Marlin and Hut Stricklin were eighth and ninth, two laps down, and Wally Dallenbach was tenth, three laps behind.

Earnhardt struggled around after repairs to his Goodwrench Chevrolet and was classified 28th. Bill Elliott, who departed with engine failure, had stood by in Dale's pit if needed to relief drive, but Dale gutted it out.

The win was Rusty's third of the season, but he did not gain a single point on leader Irvan. Ernie had led the most laps and added another huge chunk of points on Earnhardt. Dale had fallen from 62 points behind to 163 behind by the conclusion of the Dover event.

been completed, only Norm Benning and Andy Belmont were forced to go home. Mike Wallace, winner of Saturday's NASCAR Busch Series race, and Brad Teague, in Jimmy Means' Ford, took the provisional starting spots.

One of the highlights of Dover's pre-race activities was a ceremony honoring longtime car owner Bud Moore for his heroism and participation in the D-Day invasion of World War II. As the world celebrated the 50th anniversary of D-Day, the NASCAR Winston Cuppers held their own festivities for Moore, who earned five Purple Hearts and the Bronze Star in the war. He was honored

It was almost this close at the finish. Rusty Wallace pulled out a three-car-length margin over Ernie Irvan to win his third race of the season at Dover.

Fin. Pos.	Str. Pos.	Car #	Driver	Team	Fin. Pos.	Str. Pos.	Car #	Driver	Team
1	6	2	Rusty Wallace	Miller Genuine Draft Ford	22	33	14	John Andretti	Team Hagan Chevrolet
2	1	28	Ernie Irvan	Texaco Havoline Ford	23	24	98	Derrike Cope	Fingerhut Ford
3	20	25	Ken Schrader	Kodiak Chevrolet	24	36	77	Greg Sacks	USAir Ford
4	32	6	Mark Martin	Valvoline Ford	25	9	21	Morgan Shepherd	Citgo Ford
5	23	24	Jeff Gordon	DuPont Chevrolet	26	22	5	Terry Labonte	Kellogg's Corn Flakes Chevrolet
6	16	17	Darrell Waltrip	Western Auto Chevrolet	27	15	29	Steve Grissom	Diamond Ridge Chevrolet
7	34	30	Michael Waltrip	Pennzoil Pontiac	28	14	3	Dale Earnhardt	GM Goodwrench Chevrolet
8	30	4	Sterling Marlin	Kodak Film Chevrolet	29	13	18	Dale Jarrett	Interstate Batteries Chevrolet
9	38	23	Hut Stricklin	Smokin' Joe's Ford	30	17	1	Rick Mast	Skoal Classic Ford
10	27	43	Wally Dallenbach	STP Pontiac	31	5	11	Bill Elliott	Budweiser Ford
11	31	42	Kyle Petty	Mello Yello Pontiac	32	21	26	Brett Bodine	Quaker State Ford
12	40	15	Lake Speed	Quality Care Ford	33	26	8	Jeff Burton	Raybestos Brakes Ford
13	41	90	Mike Wallace	Heilig-Meyers Ford	34	8	40	Bobby Hamilton	Kendall Pontiac
14	3	41	Joe Nemechek	Meineke Mufflers Chevrolet	35	7	16	Ted Musgrave	The Family Channel Ford
15	39	19	Loy Allen	Hooters Ford	36	25	47	Billy Standridge	Johnson's Racing Ford
16	12	75	Todd Bodine	Factory Stores of America Ford	37	11	31	Ward Burton	Hardee's Chevrolet
17	10	55	Jimmy Hensley	Petron Plus Ford	38	19	32	Dick Trickle	Active Trucking Chevrolet
18	29	71	Dave Marcis	Marcis Racing Chevrolet	39	28	27	Jimmy Spencer	McDonald's Ford
19	18	10	Ricky Rudd	Tide Ford	40	42	52	Brad Teague	Means Racing Ford
20	4	22	Bobby Labonte	Maxwell House Coffee Pontiac	41	2	7	Geoff Bodine	Exide Batteries Ford
21	35	12	Chuck Bown	ReLife Ford	42	37	33	Harry Gant	Skoal Bandit Chevrolet

UAW-GM Teamwork 500

I n the midst of his winning streak last year, Mark Martin commented that "When you've got the hot horse, you ride it the best you can because you never know how long it will stay that way."

Rusty Wallace must have been paying attention.

The Miller driver rolled into Pocono flushed with his Dover success. He had run well at Charlotte, although beaten at the end by Jeff Gordon's two-tire change on pit road. But he knew his had been the car to beat at the 1.5-mile Charlotte track. The next week at Dover, he held off everything Ernie Irvan had to throw at him and conquered the Monster Mile.

Now at Drs. Joe and Rose Mattioli's 2.5-mile triangular superspeedway, Wallace was determined to continue the roll. He was 329 behind, but with a little help in the form of a poor finish by point leader Ernie Irvan, Wallace believed this was just the right place to take a big bite out of Ernie's lead.

The Dover bug had bitten Dale Earnhardt. He was only 163 behind and knew that there was a lot of racing left in the season. Still, 163 behind was unfamiliar territory for the black-clad Goodwrench crew, and no one wanted to let Ernie and the lead get much further away.

(Top) Jeff Gordon's "Rainbow Warriors" gave him great stops all day, but he couldn't handle Rusty Wallace on the race track. (Right) The weekend in the Poconos was like a honeymoon for Rusty Wallace. He started from the pole, led the most laps and won. What more could one ask for?

94

Oh my! Four-wide! Darrell Waltrip, Ernie Irvan, Sterling Marlin and Michael Waltrip head down the frontstretch to see who will lift first!

For the longest time during first-round qualifying, it appeared that Ricky Rudd would be the surprise of the session. Rudd put together a scorching lap in his Tide Ford and set the mark for the others. No one had ever cracked the 55-second mark at Pocono until Rudd's blis-tering 54.844. That one set tongues wagging on pit road — few of the drivers who had yet to qualify felt they could beat him.

Enter one black Miller Ford.

Rusty recognized the mark to beat and proceeded to

Many wondered if the race would be held as scheduled due to Sunday morning's inclement weather.

relegate Rudd to the outside of the front row by thundering around the old spinach patch in 54.692 seconds! Rudd was the first to shake Wallace's hand!

Mark Martin, also ran under the 55-second mark and claimed third place on the starting grid. Wallace and Rudd were pleased, but so was Mark. It was an outstanding team achievement with a backup car. Fourth fastest and continuing his string of good runs was Jeff Gordon, just ahead of Hendrick Motorsport teammate Ken Schrader.

Brett Bodine was sixth-fastest, just ahead of Irvan. A fleet Dick Trickle, along with Ted Musgrave and Michael Waltrip, claimed the final top 10 qualifying positions. Earnhardt qualified 19th, just ahead of Greg Sacks, who was the fastest Hoosier-shod car in the field.

With second-round qualifying a victim of day-long rains, the remainder of the field was determined by first-round times. Chuck Bown took one provisional spot in

Bobby Allison's Ford, and Bob Keselowski took the second provisional spot while behind the wheel of Jimmy Means' Ford. Billy Standridge and Andy Belmont were unable to make the field.

For a while Sunday, it appeared that the UAW-GM Teamwork 500 might run less than 500 miles — if it ran at all! Rain and fog shrouded the track all morning. Finally, the clouds lifted and the race began 90 minutes late — green and yellow flags were displayed simultaneously after 15 caution laps.

Rusty established his Ford as one of the cars

Okay, all sing on the count of three, "Rain, rain go away, come again some other day." Mike Wallace and a pair of Dales wait for driver introductions.

out the final yellow with just six laps remaining. The complexion of the race changed instantly.

The leaders headed for pit road, and all but Earnhardt (trying to steal a page from Gordon's How-to-Win-at-Charlotte book) took four tires. Andy Petree gave Earnhardt just two Goodyears, and Dale emerged from pit road in the lead. Five cars on the tail-end of the lead lap were in front of him. Wallace was behind the Goodwrench Chevrolet, and Jeff Gordon was behind Wallace. But Gordon, trying to warm his Goodyears, spun into the muck in the first turn and was mired there. He did manage to return to the track.

Wallace knew only two things: in order to win, he had to pass Earnhardt, and with only a few laps left in a race, there is no wider car on the track than the Goodwrench Chevrolet. The field hammered its way into the first turn, and Wallace dove for the bottom. His four Goodyears bit, but Dale's two couldn't duplicate the feat. Wallace pulled ahead and roared

to beat early in the race. The other was Irvan's Ford. For a while the race looked like it might become a repeat of Dover the previous week, where the two fought it out at the finish. This time, however, Irvan's chassis combination faded three-quarters of the way through the event. Then he lost a cylinder with 35 laps to go. Still, Ernie managed a seventh-place finish and maintained a large lead in the point battle after 13 races.

Wallace pulled away from the field after Ernie slowed and drew away to a 20-second (nearly a half-lap) lead over Earnhardt as the laps wound down. It looked like an easy victory until debris from Martin's cut tire brought

around to his second consecutive victory, beating Earnhardt to the line by three car-lengths. Schrader and Shepherd finished third and fourth, Martin fifth. Gordon was sixth.

Brett Bodine followed Irvan across the line. Mast and Elliott were the final drivers in the top 10.

Wallace, at the end of an 11-day odyssey, had notched his 35th career NASCAR Winston Cup victory. Following his Dover victory, the team had gone to Michigan for tests and then to Pocono for the race.

"Man, we're just going to go home and crash," said a grinning Wallace as he prepared to head for the airport.

Harry Gant was hoping that some of the old Pocono magic would surface, but he could manage only a 16th-place finish.

Fin. Pos.	Str. Pos.	Car #	Driver	Team	Fin. Pos.	Str. Pos.	Car #	Driver	Team
1	1	2	Rusty Wallace	Miller Genuine Draft Ford	22	35	8	Jeff Burton	Raybestos Brakes Ford
2	19	3	Dale Earnhardt	GM Goodwrench Chevrolet	23	33	15	Lake Speed	Quality Care Ford
3	5	25	Ken Schrader	Kodiak Chevrolet	24	20	77	Greg Sacks	USAir Ford
4	26	21	Morgan Shepherd	Citgo Ford	25	27	22	Bobby Labonte	Maxwell House Coffee Pontiac
5	3	6	Mark Martin	Valvoline Ford	26	37	29	Steve Grissom	Diamond Ridge Chevrolet
6	4	24	Jeff Gordon	DuPont Chevrolet	27	32	40	Bobby Hamilton	Kendall Pontiac
7	7	28	Ernie Irvan	Texaco Havoline Ford	28	40	9	Rich Bickle	Melling Engine Parts Ford
8	6	26	Brett Bodine	Quaker State Ford	29	17	55	Jimmy Hensley	D.R. Racing Ford
9	39	1	Rick Mast	Skoal Classic Ford	30	12	17	Darrell Waltrip	Western Auto Chevrolet
10	16	11	Bill Elliott	Budweiser Ford	31	31	19	Loy Allen	Hooters Ford
11	10	30	Michael Waltrip	Pennzoil Pontiac	32	11	41	Joe Nemechek	Meineke Mufflers Chevrolet
12	14	42	Kyle Petty	Mello Yello Pontiac	33	34	71	Dave Marcis	Mente Chevrolet
13	23	23	Hut Stricklin	Smokin' Joe's Ford	34	8	32	Dick Trickle	Active Racing Chevrolet
14	28	75	Todd Bodine	Factory Stores of America Ford	35	21	14	John Andretti	Caesars Pocono Resorts Chevrolet
15	9	16	Ted Musgrave	The Family Channel Ford	36	38	90	Mike Wallace	Heilig-Meyers Ford
16	24	33	Harry Gant	Skoal Bandit Chevrolet	37	29	27	Jimmy Spencer	McDonald's Ford
17	13	43	Wally Dallenbach	STP Pontiac	38	18	4	Sterling Marlin	Kodak Film Chevrolet
18	15	5	Terry Labonte	Kellogg's Corn Flakes Chevrolet	39	41	12	Chuck Bown	Precision Rest. Serv. Ford
19	30	7	Geoff Bodine	Exide Batteries Ford	40	36	98	Derrike Cope	Fingerhut Ford
20	22	18	Dale Jarrett	Interstate Batteries Chevrolet	41	42	52	Bob Keselowski	Means Racing Ford
21	2	10	Ricky Rudd	Tide Ford	42	25	31	Ward Burton	Hardee's Chevrolet

MILLER GENUINE DRAFT 400

MICHIGAN
INTERNATIONAL SPEEDWAY

JUNE 19, 1994

Rusty Wallace, working on a two-race winning streak, arrived at Michigan brimming with confidence. His test session the previous week with a new car, nicknamed "The Captain" in honor of team co-owner and Michigan International Speedway owner Roger Penske, had proven to be one of the best of the season for the Penske South team.

And the race was sponsored by Miller Genuine Draft, the brand proudly emblazoned on Rusty's race car and the chest of his driver's suit. After two wins and a second place in his last three races, Rusty felt his team could continue the streak.

But despite his last three finishes, Wallace had been unable to make a big dent in Ernie Irvan's point lead. Ernie had heeded the advice of Larry McReynolds and Robert Yates, and he had taken the best he could from each race. He had limped around Pocono the previous week to a seventh-place finish and brought a 135-point lead over Dale Earnhardt to Michigan. Rusty was third and trying to close the gap, but he was still 295 behind.

Right behind the top three, Mark Martin and Kenny Schrader were duking it out for fourth. Kenny had brought a 14-point advantage to MIS. Morgan Shepherd and Ricky Rudd were hanging tough in sixth and seventh, while Michael Waltrip had moved up to eighth place in the standings. Lake Speed was ninth and Kyle Petty 10th, but Jeff Gordon's win at Charlotte and strong finishes at Dover and Pocono had brought the DuPont Chevrolet driver to

(Top) Morgan Shepherd follows pole-sitter Loy Allen around the outside of Bobby Hillin (44). Morgan had the best day of the three, finishing a strong fifth. (Right) Junior Johnson devised a way to beat the Michigan heat while he watches the action from pit road. Bill Elliott fought his way to an 11th-place finish for Johnson's team.

100

Unfortunately, Geoff Bodine didn't finish at the front of the pack; he exited 22 laps from the conclusion with rear end failure. Kenny Schrader (25) finished sixth, and Dale Jarrett (18) came from 35th to finish 14th. Rusty Wallace took the lead from Dale Earnhardt with three laps remaining to post the victory.

within 10 points of Kyle.

Michigan's Miller race brought 52 teams to the two-mile oval; three of those were making test forays in preparation for the 1995 season. Kenny Wallace was on hand with a Ford from the Filmar shop that fields his NASCAR Busch series effort. Bobby Hillin was the driver for the Hardy Boys/Dawsonville Ford sponsored by Buss Fuses. That black Ford Thunderbird, prepared in the Elliott shop north of Atlanta and powered by engines from Ernie Elliott, hinted of associations to come. After all, Bill Elliott's contract with Junior Johnson would expire at the conclusion of the 1994 season!

The other new team at MIS was owned by former Ford worldwide racing boss Michael Kranefuss, who retired from FoMoCo last fall. IndyCar magnate Carl Haas was

Bobby Hillin, driving the Charles Hardy-owned Ford prepared in the Elliott shop in Dawsonville, GA, finished 16th in the Michigan race.

part-owner of the team, and crew chief Tim Brewer also had a piece of the action. The Ford (naturally!) carried the number "07" and was driven by IndyCar regular Robby Gordon. Kranefuss chose the number, in part, to honor the late NASCAR Winston Cup champion Alan Kulwicki, for whom he had gained a great deal of respect when they were both associated with Ford.

Leading the "no problem" brigade — and winning his third pole position of the season — was Hoosier-shod Loy Allen Jr., who posted a new event record of 180.641 mph despite the condition of the track.

Geoff Bodine completed a Hoosier front row, while Bill Elliott, with an engine from the Stavola Brothers (!) stuffed under his Ford's hood, qualified third fastest. Terry Labonte was fourth, ahead of Wallace, and Rudd continued his fine first season as a car owner by qualifying ahead of Gordon. Martin, Greg Sacks and Brett Bodine completed the top 10. Irvan and Earnhardt struggled, qualifying 23rd and 24th, while Jeff Purvis, in

A huge throng — guaranteed by the addition of two new grandstands which had sold out along with the rest — greeted the Cuppers as they rolled under the green. The temperature was near 100 degrees.

It was evident that Jeff Gordon and Rusty had strong cars: each led a large portion of the first half of the race. Then Wallace began to dominate; he drew away to a three-second lead over Earnhardt. Irvan had already lost a cylinder, so Wallace and Earnhardt both knew this was an excellent chance to gain points. Gordon eventually faded with an oil leak.

Forced to stay out an extra lap when the final yellow appeared for Hillin's spin (with 26 laps to go), Wallace coasted down pit road, out of fuel, for his final stop. Crew chief Buddy Parrott sprayed ether into the engine to make it fire and took a tumble when Rusty launched off pit road. Wallace had fallen to 11th place, but when the green flag flew with 19 to go, Wallace lit the afterburners. Seven laps later, he was

an infrequent outing, turned in the 13th-fastest time. Jeremy Mayfield qualified 18th. Kenny Wallace made the field in 22nd place; Hillin, 26th. Robby Gordon just squeaked the Kranefuss/Haas entry into the field. Tim Steele, driving in relief of Chuck Bown, put Bobby Allison's Ford in the 29th position for the start.

After Elliott's qualifying lap, the Stavola Brothers engine was removed from the redhead's car and installed in Jimmy Spencer's Mac Attack. Spencer went out in the second round, turned in the 12th-fastest time in the field and then watched dispiritedly as the motor was yanked from his car and stuffed back into Elliott's Bud Ford for the race.

Failing to make the tough field at MIS were: Dave Marcis, Mike Wallace, Jimmy Horton, Brad Teague, Bob Brevak, Billy Standridge, Dick Trickle, H.B. Bailey and Winston West champ Rick Carelli. And, for the fourth time this season, Petty Enterprises loaded the STP Pontiac for the long ride home.

Sterling Marlin, Ernie Irvan and Ken Schrader found some time to catch up before the start of the Miller Genuine Draft 400.

Ted Musgrave recorded the best finishing position of this foursome, taking his Family Channel Ford to a ninth-place finish.

third. With 10 laps left, he was dogging leader Earnhardt. With just over three laps to go, Rusty dove under Earnhardt and pulled away to his third consecutive win, leaving Dale to scrap with Martin for second place. Dale barely won that battle.

Irvan came home 18th. After Rusty and Dale did their calculations, they realized their weekend in Michigan had paid large dividends. Dale now trailed by only 78, and Rusty had gained 71 points to trail the Havoline Ford by only 224.

Rudd continued to impress, bringing his Tide Ford home fourth, while Shepherd beat Schrader for fifth place. Rookie Joe Nemechek was seventh, and Ted Musgrave finished sandwiched between Michael and Darrell Waltrip.

Jimmy Spencer takes to the outside to pass rookie Steve Grissom's Chevrolet. Spencer finished 23rd, Grissom, 26th.

Rusty Wallace plunked his Miller Ford at the front of the field and led the most laps on the way to his fifth victory of the season. He was delighted to win for car owner Roger Penske at Penske's two-mile Michigan track.

Fin. Pos.	Str. Pos.	Car #	Driver	Team	Fin. Pos.	Str. Pos.	Car #	Driver	Team
1	5	2	Rusty Wallace	Miller Genuine Draft Ford	22	39	23	Hut Stricklin	Smokin' Joe's Ford
2	24	3	Dale Earnhardt	GM Goodwrench Chevrolet	23	21	27	Jimmy Spencer	McDonald's Ford
3	8	6	Mark Martin	Valvoline Ford	24	1	19	Loy Allen	Hooters Ford
4	6	10	Ricky Rudd	Tide Ford	25	18	02	Jeremy Mayfield	Children's Miracle Network Ford
5	12	21	Morgan Shepherd	Citgo Ford	26	27	29	Steve Grissom	Diamond Ridge Chevrolet
6	31	25	Ken Schrader	Kodiak Chevrolet	27	18	51	Jeff Purvis	Country Time Chevrolet
7	17	41	Joe Nemechek	Meineke Mufflers Ford	28	2	7	Geoff Bodine	Exide Batteries Ford
8	11	30	Michael Waltrip	Pennzoil Pontiac	29	15	31	Ward Burton	Hardee's Chevrolet
9	40	16	Ted Musgrave	The Family Channel Ford	30	25	9	Rich Bickle	Melling Engine Parts Ford
10	34	17	Darrell Waltrip	Western Auto Chevrolet	31	36	75	Todd Bodine	Factory Stores of America Ford
11	3	11	Bill Elliott	Budweiser Ford	32	10	26	Brett Bodine	Quaker State Ford
12	7	24	Jeff Gordon	DuPont Chevrolet	33	9	77	Greg Sacks	USAir Ford
13	16	1	Rick Mast	Skoal Classic Ford	34	20	4	Sterling Marlin	Kodak Film Chevrolet
14	35	18	Dale Jarrett	Interstate Batteries Chevrolet	35	37	33	Harry Gant	Skoal Bandit Chevrolet
15	30	22	Bobby Labonte	Maxwell House Coffee Pontiac	36	33	14	John Andretti	Motorsports Design Chevrolet
16	26	44	Bobby Hillin	Buss Fuses Ford	37	14	98	Derrike Cope	Fingerhut Ford
17	41	42	Kyle Petty	Mello Yello Pontiac	38	38	07	Robby Gordon	Kranefuss-Hass Ford
18	23	28	Ernie Irvan	Texaco Havoline Ford	39	29	12	Tim Steele	Teletron Ford
19	22	81	Kenny Wallace	TIC Financial Ford	40	28	15	Lake Speed	Quality Care Ford
20	4	5	Terry Labonte	Kellogg's Corn Flakes Chevrolet	41	42	40	Bobby Hamilton	Kendall Pontiac
21	32	8	Jeff Burton	Raybestos Brakes Ford	42	19	55	Jimmy Hensley	Petron Plus Ford

PEPSI 400

DAYTONA
INTERNATIONAL SPEEDWAY

JULY 2, 1994

Rusty Wallace's three consecutive wins had not only given his team renewed hope for winning the NASCAR Winston Cup championship but had also put Ford in the lead in the Manufacturer's Championship standings. The Blue Oval bunch headed to Daytona and the Pepsi 400 a mere six markers ahead of Chevrolet. If that lead was to be extended at The Beach, most felt it would be the doings of a Ford team other than the Miller crew. After all, even Wallace was frustrated by his poor record at Daytona and Talladega.

The team expected to carry the Ford banner at Daytona was point leader Ernie Irvan, whose Robert Yates-owned Havoline rocketships could be depended upon to run at the front in restrictor-plate races. When the teams unloaded in the Daytona garage area, Irvan's point lead over Dale Earnhardt was 78. Rusty, though successful in cutting into Irvan's lead in the last four races, was still 224 in arrears.

Mark Martin now trailed by 313 and held a mere six-point lead over Kenny Schrader. Sixth-place Morgan Shepherd had issues other than point standings on his mind. Morgan had used the off-weekend between Michigan and Daytona to marry Cindy Jones. Eddie Wood, resplendent in a black tux, was Morgan's best man.

Back at the track, Ricky Rudd simply would not go away. He was seventh in the standings, just 41 points behind

(Top) Bill Elliott (11) and Mike Wallace diced for position throughout the Pepsi 400 at Daytona; Wallace came out ahead at the end of the race. Elliott finished 19th, seven positions behind Wallace. (Right) Crew chief Mike Hill makes a weight adjustment in the rear window while the remainder of the McDonald's crew finishes a four-tire change. Hill got the car right and Jimmy Spencer went on to notch his first career victory.

Lake Speed (15) came home to a 10th-place finish. Sterling Marlin (4) failed to sweep the year's races at Daytona. Loy Allen Jr. (19) qualified on the outside of the front row but lost the engine in his Hooters Ford just past quarter-distance.

Shepherd. Week after week, Rudd turned in solid performances with his new team. He was clearly the surprise of the first half of the season, and people were being forced to take his effort seriously. He had been able to work himself into contention for a victory in several races — an accomplishment most had felt he could not achieve with a first-year team.

Michael Waltrip held eighth place, just 21 points behind Rudd, and Jeff Gordon had moved into ninth place, passing Kyle Petty. There were plenty of surprises at both ends of the point table!

In the days prior to the Pepsi 400, SkyBox trading cards announced sponsorship of Dick Trickle's team at

Perfectly timed pit work is crucial to all teams and plays a key role in keeping the drivers in the position to win.

selected races, and Valvoline said it would continue to back Roush Racing and Martin for several more years. While Valvoline was re-upping, Bobby Labonte and car owner Bill Davis got the word that Maxwell House would not return as their sponsor for 1995. Doug Williams was released from his role as crew chief by the owners of the Billy Hagan Chevrolets, driven by John Andretti. Jessie Coke took over the role of head wrench.

For the longest time during qualifying, it looked like Loy Allen Jr. and his Hoosiers would start from the pole again at Daytona — then the 50th qualifier took his lap. Allen, who had run late in the February session and bumped Earnhardt from

the Daytona 500 pole, had the tables turned on him. Earnhardt drilled the best lap and plunked Goodyear on the pole for the Pepsi race.

Jimmy Spencer, who had run well in the first two restrictor-plate races, put it all together to put the Mac Attack Ford on the second row, just inside of Daytona 500 winner Sterling Marlin. Irvan and Schrader made up the third row, with Hoosier-runners Geoff Bodine and Greg Sacks claiming the seventh- and eighth-fastest laps. Terry Labonte and Jimmy Hensley completed the top 10, with Dale Jarrett, Jeff Gordon and Rusty right behind.

While Earnhardt, Allen and Spencer were celebrating their good fortunes, the nightmares continued for others. Kyle Petty was a desultory 36th; nothing seemed to be working for the Mello Yello effort. Rick Mast took a provisional, and Bobby Hamilton, in the second Sabates Pontiac, used his second-straight provisional to get in the field. Bill Elliott threw up his hands and, for the second time in five races, was forced to use the former champion's provisional.

Brad Teague, Bobby Hillin (in the Moroso Ford), Joe Ruttman, Billy Standridge and Delma Cowart all failed to get in, and the STP crew loaded the Petty Enterprises Pontiac into its transporter.

Junior Johnson's teams had started 90 races since one of his Fords had gone to victory lane (the final race of the 1992 season). Most expected Bill Elliott to be the driver who would break the slump for Junior during the 1994 season; Jimmy Spencer was considered a driver for the future. No one expected the Pepsi 400 victory lane to become a McDonald's drive-through!

But on sultry Florida days in July, anything can happen.

In mid-race action at Daytona, Ricky Rudd takes his Tide Ford to the high side to pass Dick Trickle's SkyBox Chevrolet.

(Above) Michael Waltrip (30), Mike Wallace (90) and Bill Elliott complete the triumvirate on the frontstretch in the Pepsi 400. Jimmy Spencer waits to see what will happen in front of him. (Left) Loy Allen Jr. was all smiles after qualifying. He claimed the outside of the front row for the Pepsi race, which fit nicely with his Daytona 500 pole position.

Ask Greg Sacks about 1985!

The Pepsi 400 was typical restrictor-plate, freight-train racing. As the race unfolded, Earnhardt, Irvan, Martin, Marlin and Gordon clearly demonstrated that they had the dominant cars. And in the second half, Earnhardt and Irvan waged their own war for supremacy. Throughout the day, however, crew chief Mike Hill had worked on the handling of Spencer's Ford. On the final caution, Hill got it right. Irvan had stopped for four fresh Goodyears and was just ahead of Spencer on the final restart. Both were out of the top 10 but steamrolled toward the front. Ernie made it all the way to the point, passing Earnhardt in just nine laps. Spencer moved up the line, one by one, towards Ernie and Dale. Spencer, following Schrader, moved past Earnhardt with 12 laps

to go when Dale slid high in the second turn.

Then Jimmy moved past Kenny with 11 to go and clamped on Irvan's bumper. He worried Ernie for the next 10 laps. On the final lap, Spencer went high in the second turn to pull even and then swept past Irvan down the backstretch.

Jeff Gordon muscled his way to eighth place in the Pepsi 400, but Rusty Wallace's poor Daytona luck continued with a lap-down, 26th-place finish.

"Mr. Excitement" lived up to his nickname as he and Irvan played 200-mph tag the remainder of the lap. Spencer beat Ernie to the flag by less than a half-car-length for his first win in what was also the most exciting finish in the first half of the NASCAR Winston Cup season. Earnhardt finished third, ahead of Martin and Schrader, with Geoff Bodine sixth, the best Hoosier finish. Younger brother Todd Bodine had a great race to finish seventh, ahead of Gordon, Shepherd and Lake Speed. Rusty had handling problems and watched his hard-earned point gains of the last three races disappear.

There's nothing like a youngster to keep a winner's britches from getting too big. Following his victory lane celebration, David Spencer asked dad Jimmy where they were going next. "Over there," dad said, pointing. "Up there to the press box for interviews. It's a place you've never been before!"

Without missing a beat David replied, "Well, you haven't ever been there, either, you know!"

It might have been the first trip to the interview room for Spencer and his son, but no one expected it to be his last. Finally, there were teeth in the Mac Attack!

Jimmy Spencer's excitement about his first Winston Cup victory was evident in victory lane.

Fin. Pos.	Str. Pos.	Car #	Driver	Team	Fin. Pos.	Str. Pos.	Car #	Driver	Team
1	3	27	Jimmy Spencer	McDonald's Ford	23	39	98	Derrike Cope	Fingerhut Ford
2	5	28	Ernie Irvan	Texaco Havoline Ford	24	42	40	Bobby Hamilton	Kendall Pontiac
3	1	3	Dale Earnhardt	GM Goodwrench Chevrolet	25	37	17	Darrell Waltrip	Western Auto Chevrolet
4	4	6	Mark Martin	Valvoline Ford	26	13	2	Rusty Wallace	Miller Genuine Draft Ford
5	6	25	Ken Schrader	Kodiak Chevrolet	27	32	71	Dave Marcis	Olive Garden Chevrolet
6	7	7	Geoff Bodine	Exide Batteries Ford	28	4	4	Sterling Marlin	Kodak Film Chevrolet
7	17	75	Todd Bodine	Factory Stores of America Ford	29	41	1	Rick Mast	Skoal Classic Ford
8	12	24	Jeff Gordon	DuPont Chevrolet	30	30	02	Jeremy Mayfield	Children's Miracle Network Ford
9	24	21	Morgan Shepherd	Citgo Ford	31	26	33	Harry Gant	Skoal Bandit Chevrolet
10	33	15	Lake Speed	Quality Care Ford	32	10	55	Jimmy Hensley	RaDiUs Motorsports Ford
11	11	18	Dale Jarrett	Interstate Batteries Chevrolet	33	21	29	Steve Grissom	Diamond Ridge Chevrolet
12	18	90	Mike Wallace	Heilig-Meyers Ford	34	36	42	Kyle Petty	Mello Yello Pontiac
13	23	30	Michael Waltrip	Pennzoil Pontiac	35	28	14	John Andretti	Financial World Chevrolet
14	16	16	Ted Musgrave	The Family Channel Ford	36	40	31	Ward Burton	Hardee's Chevrolet
15	9	5	Terry Labonte	Kellogg's Corn Flakes Chevrolet	37	8	77	Greg Sacks	USAir Ford
16	22	26	Brett Bodine	Quaker State Ford	38	19	51	Jeff Purvis	Country Time Chevrolet
17	31	10	Ricky Rudd	Tide Ford	39	38	41	Joe Nemechek	Meineke Mufflers Chevrolet
18	27	8	Jeff Burton	Raybestos Brakes Ford	40	2	19	Loy Allen	Hooters Ford
19	43	11	Bill Elliott	Budweiser Ford	41	35	53	Ritchie Petty	Maurice Petty Ford
20	34	9	Rich Bickle	Melling Racing Ford	42	20	23	Hut Stricklin	Smokin' Joe's Ford
21	25	32	Dick Trickle	SkyBox International Chevrolet	43	29	12	Tim Steele	ReLife Ford
22	14	22	Bobby Labonte	Maxwell House Coffee Pontiac					

SLICK 50 300

With half the season in the books, teams used the few days between the Pepsi 400 and New Hampshire's Slick 50 300 to evaluate their seasons and take a long, hard look at what needed to be done in the second half of the year.

For some, it was painful. Many who, at the beginning of the season, had expected to challenge for the championship now found themselves on the brink of disaster. Others who had every expectation of landing in the top 10 in points instead found themselves outside the top 20, facing a hard, uphill battle to get to 15th or better by the season's end.

Kyle Petty, who finished fifth in last year's standings, had posted only three top five finishes in the first half of the year and was 12th in points. Sterling Marlin, winner of the Daytona 500, had had only one other top 10 finish and was 14th. Terry Labonte, the North Wilkesboro winner, was 15th in points but had posted only two other top 10 finishes. Dale Jarrett, who finished fourth in points last year, was having a nightmarish season. After the first half of 1994, he was 16th.

The Redhead was caught in a dismal string that seemed to have no end. Bill Elliott had gone more than one-and-a-half seasons without a win and had only one top five finish this year. He was 17th, just ahead of Geoff Bodine, who

(Top) Rick Mast battled Joe Nemechek in the early part of the Slick 50 300, but when it came time to appear at the pay window, Mast was ninth and Nemechek 19th. (Right) Car owner and driver Ricky Rudd and crew-chief Billy Ingle exude the joy of victory after their first win together. Rudd beat nemesis Dale Earnhardt in a seven-lap sprint at the end.

Michael Waltrip's luck continued to sour. He exited mid-way through the race with a broken oil pump.

team, and at the half, the Skoal group was a disappointing 19th. Bobby Labonte had struggled. Brett Bodine had continued his strong qualifying showings but had produced only three top 10s. He was 21st in points, just behind Bobby. Jimmy Spencer climbed to 26th after his Pepsi 400 victory, but that win had been the highlight of his season.

Harry Gant and his team simply could not make his Chevrolets handle, and Gant, now 28th in points, was having a very difficult final season. Derrike Cope, despite his new Fingerhut sponsorship, could not get Cale Yarborough's Fords to the finish line. Wally Dallenbach and Richard Petty were unbelievably disappointed; they were 33rd in points.

Obviously, some things had to happen. Darrell Waltrip, frustrated by his 13th position in the standings,

had tied his fortunes to the success or failure of Hoosier tires. Thus far, with the exception of winning the Winston Select, Bodine's season had been a dismal collection of poor results.

Last year's bad luck was still following Rick Mast's

Crew chief Tony Glover presses the mike button on his headset to talk with Sterling Marlin as the Morgan-McClure crew services the Kodak Chevrolet. Their combined efforts resulted in 10th place.

114

A strong-running Morgan Shepherd takes the Wood Brothers' Citgo Ford around the outside of Darrell Waltrip's Western Auto Chevrolet. Shepherd went on to finish in sixth place while Darrell came home a lap down in 23rd place.

fired the first shot. He dismissed his crew chief and engine-builder.

Bobby Allison named Tim Steele to drive his Fords.

Ward Burton's team named Phillippe Lopez as crew chief for the Hardee's Chevrolet. As expected, Robin Pemberton returned to Roush Racing. Pemberton took over as head wrench for Ted Musgrave's effort.

Ernie Irvan brought an 88-point lead to New Hampshire. The race for the NASCAR Winston Cup was beginning to look like a battle between Irvan and his closest pursuer, Dale Earnhardt. Rusty Wallace had fallen behind by 319 points, and Mark Martin was now 428 in arrears, just 16 points ahead of Kenny Schrader.

After qualifying had been completed at Bahre's speed

Despite a ding in the left front of his Tide Ford, Ricky Rudd would not be denied at New Hampshire. He had the answer for everyone, including Dale Earnhardt.

115

already taken a beating from the sticky tires, heavy cars and near 100-degree weather. Jeff Gordon took the outside of the front row, and Ricky Rudd sparkled with the third-fastest lap. Rudd came in just ahead of a surprising fourth-place qualifier, Bobby Labonte. Schrader and Musgrave were fifth and sixth ahead of Marlin and Cope. Both Marlin and Cope hoped to get something going. Morgan Shepherd and Martin completed the top 10. Kyle and Steele took the provisionals. So Dallenbach went home, as did Loy Allen, Robert Pressley, Joe Bessey and Jamie Aube.

Few knew what to expect Sunday. The race turned into one of survival with 17 cautions for 83 of the 300 laps. The pavement continued to take a beating, as did the machinery, which lost battle after battle. Irvan led the most laps but spun on a restart with 24 laps to go. He finished 30th and could only watch as his point lead shrunk.

During the final yellow of the day, a quick two-tire stop by the Tide crew put Rudd back on the track behind Earnhardt, who looked ready to win on the four new Goodyears his "Flying Aces" had given him. But Rudd had other ideas.

After the green flag dropped, Earnhardt hammered into the first turn but slipped just enough to let Rudd alongside. The two old rivals traded paint, sheetmetal and bondo. Finally, Rudd grunted his way past and held off Earnhardt for the

palace, doubters no longer wondered why Irvan was at the head of the point standings. He set a new lap record with his run around the one-mile oval, and the track had

Ernie Irvan, after contending for the win throughout the race, ended his day and hopes for victory in a wreck which occurred while he was preparing for a restart.

final five laps.

Ricky the car owner congratulated Ricky the driver in victory lane. It was the first win for a new team that had been given little consideration at the beginning of the season.

Wallace was right behind Earnhardt, and both posted big gains on Irvan, with Dale taking the point lead.

Martin also gained on Irvan with a fourth place finish, and Todd Bodine notched his first career top-five finish. Musgrave (with Pemberton making the calls for the first time) finished seventh, just behind Shepherd. Kyle Petty, Mast and Marlin were all grinning after claiming the final top-10 positions. A total of 18 cars had finished on the lead lap at the tour's northernmost stop of the year.

Ricky Rudd receives his first Gatorade dousing as a victorious car owner/driver after winning at New Hampshire.

Fin. Pos.	Str. Pos.	Car #	Driver	Team	Fin. Pos.	Str. Pos.	Car #	Driver	Team
1	3	10	Ricky Rudd	Tide Ford	22	40	34	Mike McLaughlin	Coors Chevrolet
2	28	3	Dale Earnhardt	GM Goodwrench Chevrolet	23	14	17	Darrell Waltrip	Western Auto Chevrolet
3	18	2	Rusty Wallace	Miller Genuine Draft Ford	24	5	25	Ken Schrader	Kodiak Chevrolet
4	10	6	Mark Martin	Valvoline Ford	25	27	77	Greg Sacks	USAir Ford
5	15	75	Todd Bodine	Factory Stores of America Ford	26	37	02	Jeremy Mayfield	Children's Miracle Network Ford
6	9	21	Morgan Shepherd	Citgo Ford	27	24	14	John Andretti	Financial World Chevrolet
7	6	16	Ted Musgrave	The Family Channel Ford	28	36	90	Mike Wallace	Heilig-Meyers Ford
8	41	42	Kyle Petty	Mello Yello Pontiac	29	20	55	Jimmy Hensley	D-R Racing Ford
9	22	1	Rick Mast	Skoal Classic Ford	30	1	28	Ernie Irvan	Texaco Havoline Ford
10	7	4	Sterling Marlin	Kodak Film Chevrolet	31	16	7	Geoff Bodine	Exide Batteries Ford
11	11	5	Terry Labonte	Kellogg's Corn Flakes Chevrolet	32	13	27	Jimmy Spencer	McDonald's Ford
12	23	26	Brett Bodine	Quaker State Ford	33	25	29	Steve Grissom	Diamond Ridge Chevrolet
13	4	22	Bobby Labonte	Maxwell House Coffee Pontiac	34	29	32	Dick Trickle	SkyBox International Chevrolet
14	31	18	Dale Jarrett	Interstate Batteries Chevrolet	35	8	98	Derrike Cope	Fingerhut Ford
15	34	15	Lake Speed	Quality Care Ford	36	30	23	Hut Stricklin	Smokin' Joe's Ford
16	21	11	Bill Elliott	Budweiser Ford	37	12	30	Michael Waltrip	Pennzoil Pontiac
17	32	33	Harry Gant	Skoal Bandit Chevrolet	38	39	8	Jeff Burton	Raybestos Brakes Ford
18	17	71	Dave Marcis	AEL Chevrolet	39	2	24	Jeff Gordon	DuPont Chevrolet
19	35	41	Joe Nemechek	Meineke Muffler Chevrolet	40	38	40	Bobby Hamilton	Kendall Pontiac
20	19	20	Randy LaJoie	Fina Lube Ford	41	42	12	Tim Steele	ReLife Ford
21	26	9	Rich Bickle	Melling Engine Parts Ford	42	33	31	Ward Burton	Hardee's Chevrolet

MILLER GENUINE DRAFT 500

POCONO
INTERNATIONAL RACEWAY

JULY 17, 1994

It had been three months since Dale Earnhardt and his Goodwrench team had come to a track as the leaders of the NASCAR Winston Cup point standings. But the black-clad team that rolled the Chevrolet from the transporter for the second visit to the Mattioli's spread in the Pocono Mountains of Pennsylvania now owned that lead — albeit a slim one.

(Top) Ted Musgrave (16) and Hut Stricklin recorded less-than-satisfactory performances at Pocono; Musgrave finished 32nd, Stricklin, 22nd. (Right) Geoff Bodine dominated the Miller Genuine Draft 500 at Pocono and posted a 1.26-second victory over Ward Burton.

Earnhardt's second place at New Hampshire, coupled with Ernie Irvan's 30th-place finish, moved the six-time champion four points ahead of the Texaco Havoline driver. Irvan's poor finish had enabled Rusty Wallace and Mark Martin to gnaw away at the lead as well — Wallace was now 241 behind and Martin was trailing by 256.

Barry Dodson, who had been released from his position as Darrell Waltrip's crew chief, showed up in a black shirt emblazoned with Mello Yello's neon colors. Car owner Felix Sabates, trying to get Kyle Petty's Pontiac back to the front of the pack, had hired Dodson as a consultant for Sabco Racing.

Brett Bodine surprised some in the garage by saying he would not return to the Quaker State Ford for the 1995 season; he was now entertaining offers for his services for next year. Bobby Allison, tired of the black cars he had fielded all season, brought a red, white and gold "12" car for Tim Steele.

Derrike Cope, released the day after the New Hampshire race, was not in his familiar seat in Cale Yarborough's car. Yarborough hired young Jeremy Mayfield from the T.W. Taylor Ford to take Cope's place. Meanwhile, Derrike found

Darrell Waltrip struggled throughout the day and could manage only 28th place.

himself in the Taylor Ford for the Pocono race.

Many expected Pocono to be the track where Hoosier scored a breakthrough in the tire battle. Judging from the qualifying results, the Indiana tire company had brought its good stuff to the 2.5-mile, triangular superspeedway.

Geoff Bodine scorched the track for a new event record with a qualifying speed of more than 163.8 miles per hour on the untested tires and led a 1-2-3-4 sweep

for the Purple H brand. It was a huge improvement for the tire company since the first Pocono race, where the best Hoosier-shod qualifier was 20th.

Right alongside Geoff, in the Exide Ford, was Ward Burton and his Hardee's Chevrolet. On the second row were Greg Sacks in the USAir Ford and Jeff Burton with the Stavola Brothers' Raybestos Ford. The fastest Goodyear-runner was Ernie Irvan, at fifth. Ricky Rudd and Jeff Gordon were sixth and seventh, ahead of Loy Allen, Ken Schrader and Rusty Wallace.

Martin qualified 12th, but Earnhardt struggled, barely making it into the first round with only the 20th-fastest time. Mayfield qualified 22nd in his first outing for Yarborough, and Cope put the Taylor Ford in 27th place on the grid. Michael Waltrip and Daytona Pepsi 400 winner Jimmy Spencer were forced to take provisionals. Jimmy Hensley, Dick Trickle, Phil Parsons and Jerry O'Neil did not turn laps fast enough to make the field.

When the race began Sunday, some concern was voiced about whether or not the Hoosiers would be good for enough laps to make using them worthwhile,

Hut Stricklin tests the outside line around turn three as he and Ted Musgrave gather steam for Pocono's extended front straight.

but that question immediately was answered when Bodine and the Burtons went to the front and stayed there. In fact, the only time Goodyear-shod cars led the Miller 500 was during caution laps or when a Goodyear team would turn its car off pit road into the lead. A Goodyear-shod car never passed a Hoosier-shod car on the track for the lead!

Geoff Bodine dominated the race on his Hoosiers, leading more laps than any other driver ever had in the history of NASCAR Winston Cup competition at the track.

The Chemung, NY, native led 156 of the 200 laps on the way to his first victory in a NASCAR Winston Cup race as a car owner.

For nearly half the race, it appeared that Bodine might have to play second fiddle to Harry Gant. Geoff and Harry were the class of the field. For 80 laps, the two streaked away from everyone else, building more than a 20-second lead over the rest of the pack. It was obvious that Gant was just cruising behind Geoff. Although Gant had struggled with the car throughout the season, he clearly now had his Skoal Chevrolet handling.

race. Irvan exited with a broken timing chain on lap 136 Martin lost his engine with 25 laps remaining, and just four laps later, Rusty's hopes of winning the Miller race faded due to a sick engine.

The race ended, as so many past Pocono races have,

After Harry Gant easily ran just behind Geoff Bodine for half the race, his hopes for a victory came to an end with a broken oil fitting.

But just past halfway, an oil fitting broke on the Skoal Chevrolet, and Harry spun in the third turn, ending his hopes for victory. As Gant's dreams of victory vanished, Bodine continued to streak away from the field. Just 30 laps later, his main adversaries started dropping out of the

with teams trying to stretch their gas mileage to the last drop. But all would be forced to pit before the finish — Bodine's Exide Ford made its final stop for a splash of fuel (three seconds worth) with 10 laps to go. He returned in third place behind Ward Burton and Joe Nemechek but

Ernie Irvan battled with Geoff Bodine early in the race but later departed with a broken timing chain.

passed Nemechek with seven laps remaining in the event.

With five laps to go, Geoff moved past Burton and the Hardee's Chevrolet and pulled away to a 1.26-second victory over the young Virginia driver. Burton and Nemechek finished second and third, and Jeff Burton finished fourth. It was the best showing of the season for all three rookie contenders. Morgan Shepherd was the first Goodyear finisher, taking fifth with the Citgo Ford, while Ricky Rudd finished sixth, ahead of Dale Earnhardt, the final car on the lead lap. Jeff Gordon was eighth, and Wallace nursed his ailing Ford home to a ninth-place finish ahead of Dale Jarrett.

Michael Waltrip was no match for the second-place Ward Burton. Waltrip finished two laps down to the leaders in his Pennzoil Pontiac.

Tim Steele was unable to debut Bobby Allison Motorsports' new colors at Pocono. Steele finished well down the list in a backup Ford.

Earnhardt, when his own seventh place and Martin's 31st-place finish were combined, had solidified his point lead. Dale now led fourth-place Martin by 326 markers and had picked up three points on Wallace to boost his margin to 244. His big gain, however, came over Irvan, who finished 37th due to a broken motor in the Texaco Ford. Earnhardt now led Ernie by 93 as the teams began preparations for the final restrictor-plate race of the season.

Geoff Bodine and his team, standing in victory lane at Pocono, paused for a moment during the celebration. Former team owner Alan Kulwicki had celebrated his last Winston Cup victory here with many of the same team members on his way to the 1992 NASCAR Winston Cup Championship.

This Pocono win meant something extra-special to each member of the "7" team.

Fin. Pos.	Str. Pos.	Car #	Driver	Team	Fin. Pos.	Str. Pos.	Car #	Driver	Team
1	1	7	Geoff Bodine	Exide Batteries Ford	22	35	23	Hut Stricklin	Smokin' Joe's Ford
2	2	31	Ward Burton	Hardee's Chevrolet	23	16	40	Bobby Hamilton	Kendall Pontiac
3	11	41	Joe Nemechek	Meineke Mufflers Chevrolet	24	42	27	Jimmy Spencer	McDonald's Ford
4	4	8	Jeff Burton	Raybestos Brakes Ford	25	36	14	John Andretti	Team Hagan Chevrolet
5	33	21	Morgan Shepherd	Citgo Ford	26	34	71	Dave Marcis	Precision Rest Services Chevrolet
6	6	10	Ricky Rudd	Tide Ford	27	37	42	Kyle Petty	Mello Yello Pontiac
7	20	3	Dale Earnhardt	GM Goodwrench Chevrolet	28	26	17	Darrell Waltrip	Western Auto Chevrolet
8	7	24	Jeff Gordon	DuPont Chevrolet	29	39	29	Steve Grissom	Diamond Ridge Chevrolet
9	10	2	Rusty Wallace	Miller Genuine Draft Ford	30	25	90	Mike Wallace	Heilig-Meyers Ford
10	17	18	Dale Jarrett	Interstate Batteries Chevrolet	31	12	6	Mark Martin	Valvoline Ford
11	31	75	Todd Bodine	Factory Stores of America Ford	32	32	16	Ted Musgrave	The Family Channel Ford
12	18	4	Sterling Marlin	Kodak Film Chevrolet	33	29	12	Tim Steele	ReLife Ford
13	13	22	Bobby Labonte	Maxwell House Coffee Pontiac	34	38	9	Rich Bickle	Melling Engine Parts Ford
14	41	30	Michael Waltrip	Pennzoil Pontiac	35	14	26	Brett Bodine	Quaker State Ford
15	28	5	Terry Labonte	Kellogg's Corn Flakes Chevrolet	36	3	77	Greg Sacks	USAir Ford
16	21	43	Wally Dallenbach	STP Pontiac	37	5	28	Ernie Irvan	Texaco Havoline Ford
17	19	11	Bill Elliott	Budweiser Ford	38	15	33	Harry Gant	Skoal Bandit Chevrolet
18	8	19	Loy Allen	Hooters Ford	39	9	25	Ken Schrader	Kodiak Chevrolet
19	27	02	Derrike Cope	Children's Miracle Network Ford	40	24	1	Rick Mast	Skoal Classic Ford
20	40	15	Lake Speed	Quality Care Ford	41	22	47	Billy Standridge	Standridge Auto Parts Ford
21	23	98	Jeremy Mayfield	Fingerhut Ford	42	30	57	Bob Schacht	Kenova Golf Construction Ford

DIEHARD 500

TALLADEGA SUPERSPEEDWAY

JULY 24, 1994

ollowing their Pepsi 400 victory, McDonald's crew chief Mike Hill watched, eagle-eyed, as the engine was torn down in Junior Johnson's shop, and the manifold was taken off the block. He took the manifold, put it in a closet and locked it away. After clicking the padlock he secured the key — the only key— in a safe place.

He was taking no chance that the manifold would disappear! After all, it was the only manifold to power a Junior Johnson car to victory during the last 90 races. With the DieHard 500 coming up — the final time the cars would run with restrictor plates in 1994 — Hill wanted to be sure his driver, Jimmy Spencer, had the best chance possible for victory at Grant Lynch's Talladega Superspeedway.

Ironically, the manifold had been built by Steve Stahr, who worked for Jack Roush's team until 1991, went to work at Junior's beginning in 1992 and then left mid-season this year to return to Roush's shop.

So when the gates opened for the DieHard 500, Spencer was bopping around the garage, very aware that he had an excellent chance to win again. Spencer would run with the same powerplant he had used to take the McDonald's Ford to victory at Daytona. The car had not been touched since then, other than to put it on jackstands in a corner of

(Top) Hut Stricklin takes his Camel Ford to the point while a pack of contenders behind him battles for the chance to overtake the position he holds. Behind Stricklin are: Ricky Rudd, Greg Sacks, Bobby Labonte, Todd Bodine, Jeff Burton, Morgan Shepherd and Kyle Petty. (Right) Jimmy Spencer gets a "cool-off" dousing after winning the DieHard 500 at Talladega, his second victory in the last four races.

124

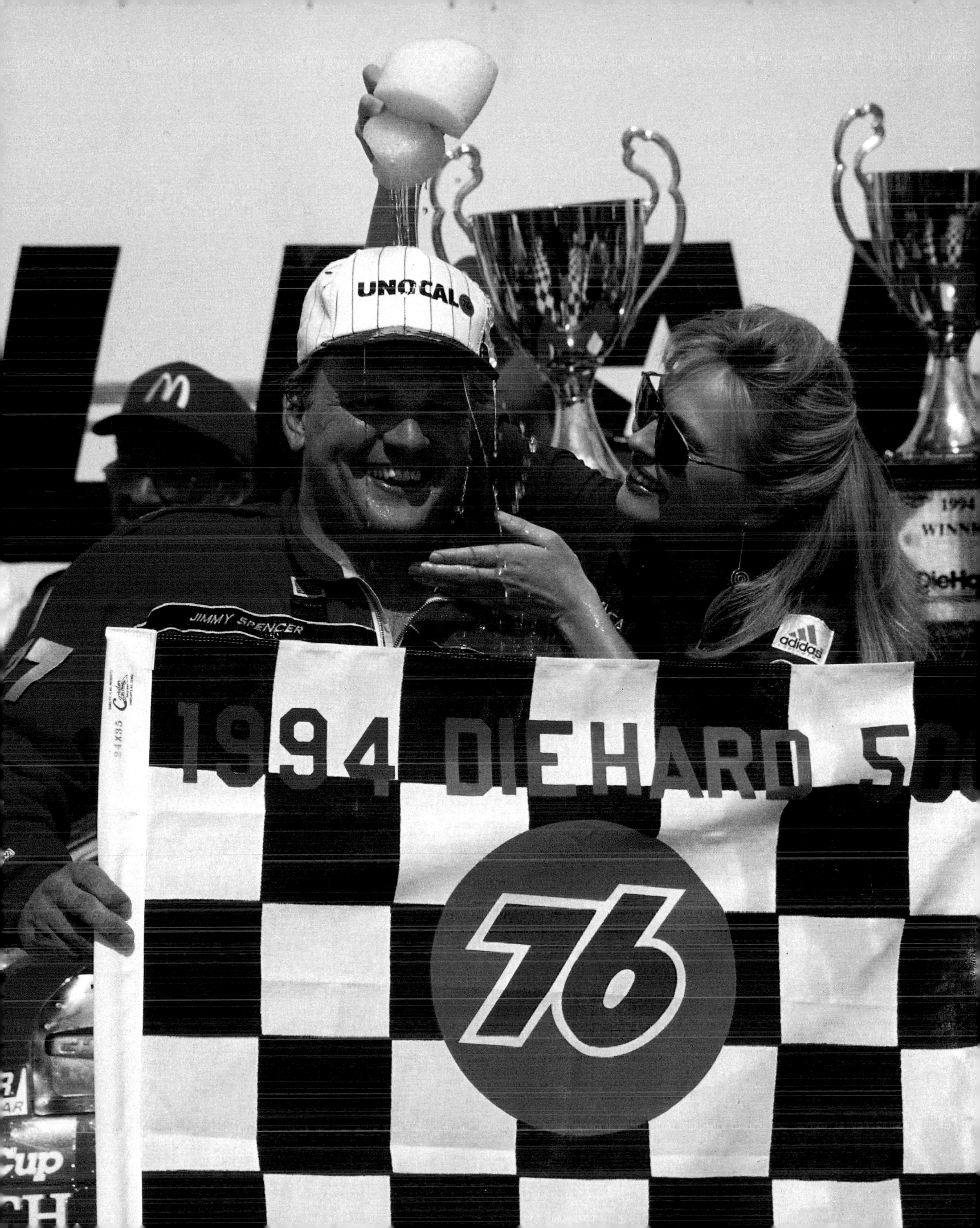
UNOCAL
JIMMY SPENCER
1994 DIEHARD 50
76
1994
WINN
adidas

Racing at Talladega always produces some of the wildest action of the year. Here, Kenny Wallace (44), Tim Steele (12) and Hut Stricklin stack it three wide.

the garage. Ernie Irvan's tire-marks from the dash to the Pepsi flag were even still visible.

Despite the juice in the Mac Attack's motor, it became clear during qualifying at the mammoth oval that it wouldn't be enough. Dale Earnhardt, determined to prove his Chevrolet had what it took to continue its big-track supremacy, took his second-straight restrictor plate pole by more than a tenth of a second over the red Ford. Earnhardt had qualified second for the Daytona 500 and fourth for the Winston 500 at Talladega earlier in the season.

Behind the front row of Goodyear-runners was Loy

Allen, showing yet again that his Hooters Ford, on its Hoosiers, was extremely fast at the tracks. His lap (third-fastest) was the first time the Ford had not qualified on the front row in a restrictor-plate race in 1994! Kenny Schrader notched the fourth-fastest lap, ahead of Ernie Irvan and Mark Martin. Todd Bodine had a super qualifying run to take seventh, ahead of Daytona 500 winner Sterling Marlin and Michael Waltrip. Wally Dallenbach pleased the STP team and car owner Richard Petty by qualifying 10th.

After crashing Bobby Allison's red, white and gold car in practice the first two times out, Tim Steele finally gave

Jeff Gordon (24) led this group of cars but later exited the race with engine failure.

qualifying were: Rich Bickle, Dick Trickle, Ritchie Petty, Derrike Cope, Ward Burton, Ben Hess, Billy Standridge, Joe Ruttman, Delma Cowart and Ronnie Sanders.

The opening laps of the race looked like an Earnhardt-Marlin battle. The two Chevrolet drivers traded the lead six times in the first 20 laps. Spencer had faded from the point but hoped his team could make adjustments to improve the handling of his Ford during pit stops. Teammate Bill Elliott moved to the front and established himself as a contender early in the race.

But all eyes in the grandstands were glued on the black Chevrolet — Earnhardt seemed determined to run at the point. He had returned to the front by quarter-distance and led until the 80th lap of the 188-lap affair, when he fell from competition with a burned piston.

His departure opened the door for the rest of the field; soon Irvan, Schrader and Elliott proved they had all they needed under their hoods. While those three shared the

the Ford's new look its first race start. Rusty Wallace continued to struggle and qualified 26th, unable to turn his restrictor-plate fortunes around. Geoff Bodine, who had dominated the week before, could only turn the 20th-fastest lap in qualifying.

Bobby Hamilton and Joe Nemechek were forced to take provisional starting spots. The drivers who failed to make the field during the sauna-like conditions of second-day

Jeremy Mayfield, in his second race with Cale Yarborough's team, watched his Fingerhut Ford come home on the hook after he was involved in a wreck.

Darrell Waltrip had hoped his luck would turn around at Talladega, but he finished 24th despite good service from his crew.

front of the pack for the next 90 laps, Spencer's crew gradually got his Ford into racing trim. During the final caution flag, with just 24 laps to go, Mike Hill and his crew found the right combination. They bumped the rear spoiler up a couple of degrees and adjusted the set-up.

And, in Spencer's words, "That sucker just flat took off and got awesome!"

Indeed.

He was third behind Irvan and Elliott when the green fell for the final time, and it took him just four laps to blow past both to take the lead with 18 laps to go. He may have been the leader, but he knew he would not go unchallenged. On the last circuit, Spencer blocked "teammate" Elliott on the backstretch and then kept the Budweiser Ford at bay through the trioval to win his second race of the last four outings.

Behind Elliott, whose drive was vintage Redhead stuff, came Irvan, who was ahead of Schrader, Marlin,

Martin and Rudd. Completing the top 10 were Dallenbach, Kenny Wallace (in the "Dawsonville Ford" prepared by the Elliott shop) and Terry Labonte.

Wallace's "big-track" luck went from bad to worse. His Miller Ford ate a piston just eight laps into the race, so Rusty was forced to make an early exit from Talladega.

The combination of finishes by Earnhardt (34th), Wallace (42nd), Irvan (3rd) and Martin (6th) gave the point chase a different look as the teams began their "week off" to prepare for the Brickyard 400.

Irvan had moved back into the lead with a 16-point margin over Earnhardt. Martin had moved past Wallace for third place but trailed Ernie by 258. Wallace was now 289 points behind the leader.

Looking as though he just stepped from an "Ultra-Tide" commercial, Dale Earnhardt heads for his car for the start of the DieHard 500.

*Bill Elliott (11) and Sterling Marlin (4) get the better of this battle with Michael Waltrip at the end of the race.
Elliott finished second, Sterling fifth and Michael 11th.*

Fin. Pos.	Str. Pos.	Car #	Driver	Team	Fin. Pos.	Str. Pos.	Car #	Driver	Team
1	2	27	Jimmy Spencer	McDonald's Ford	22	41	40	Bobby Hamilton	Kendall Pontiac
2	11	11	Bill Elliott	Budweiser Ford	23	32	20	Bobby Hillin	Fina Lube Ford
3	5	28	Ernie Irvan	Texaco Havoline Ford	24	22	17	Darrell Waltrip	Western Auto Chevrolet
4	4	25	Ken Schrader	Kodiak Chevrolet	25	37	23	Hut Stricklin	Smokin' Joe's Ford
5	8	4	Sterling Marlin	Kodak Film Chevrolet	26	39	8	Jeff Burton	Raybestos Brakes Ford
6	6	6	Mark Martin	Valvoline Ford	27	34	71	Dave Marcis	STG Chevrolet
7	28	10	Ricky Rudd	Tide Ford	28	40	52	Brad Teague	Moanc Racing Ford
8	10	43	Wally Dallenbach	STP Pontiac	29	29	77	Greg Sacks	USAir Ford
9	16	44	Kenny Wallace	Buss Fuses Ford	30	36	55	Jimmy Hensley	RaDIUs Ford
10	12	5	Terry Labonte	Kellogg's Corn Flakes Chevrolet	31	15	24	Jeff Gordon	DuPont Chevrolet
11	9	30	Michael Waltrip	Pennzoil Pontiac	32	25	98	Jeremy Mayfield	Fingerhut Ford
12	35	22	Bobby Labonte	Maxwell House Coffee Pontiac	33	20	7	Geoff Bodine	Exide Batteries Ford
13	14	90	Mike Wallace	Heilig-Meyers Ford	34	1	3	Dale Earnhardt	GM Goodwrench Chevrolet
14	18	15	Lake Speed	Quality Care Ford	35	42	41	Joe Nemechek	Meineke Mufflers Chevrolet
15	31	21	Morgan Shepherd	Citgo Ford	36	40	51	Jeff Purvis	Country Time Chevrolet
16	7	75	Todd Bodine	Factory Stores of America Ford	37	3	19	Loy Allen	Hooters Ford
17	19	26	Brett Bodine	Quaker State Ford	38	27	12	Tim Steel	ReLife Ford
18	24	29	Steve Grissom	Diamond Ridge Chevrolet	39	13	18	Dale Jarrett	Interstate Batteries Chevrolet
19	23	42	Kyle Petty	Mello Yello Pontiac	40	21	14	John Andretti	Financial World Chevrolet
20	38	1	Rick Mast	Skoal Classic Ford	41	17	16	Ted Musgrave	The Family Channel Ford
21	33	33	Harry Gant	Skoal Bandit Chevrolet	42	26	2	Rusty Wallace	Miller Genuine Draft Ford

BRICKYARD 400

INDIANAPOLIS
MOTOR SPEEDWAY

AUGUST 6, 1994

F inally, after more than two years of preparation, the most ballyhooed and long-awaited event in the history of NASCAR racing was about to begin.

Ernie Irvan may have been the point leader as the teams rolled up the interstates, but at the moment, the series as a whole — and one event in particular— was the focus of the world's motorsports enthusiasts.

The inaugural running of the Brickyard 400 — sold out within 12 hours of the ticket deadline a year before — guaranteed the largest crowd ever to see a NASCAR Winston Cup race. More than 300,000 fans were on hand to witness history in the making as the Cup cars rolled out of Gasoline Alley for their first official forays around the 2.5-mile oval.

Two weeks prior to the race, one of the most unusual press conferences in NASCAR history had been held at Talladega. Large numbers of midwestern media members were in attendance to obtain advance material for the Brickyard race, but what made the event so unusual was that Talladega officials had allowed their track to be used as

(Top) With only one lap complete and his number not yet posted at the top of the leader board, Rick Mast streaks into the first turn in the lead. Dale Earnhardt had already fallen to fourth place. (Right) Jeff Gordon celebrated his return to Indiana, where he lived for several years, with a victory in the inaugural Brickyard 400.

the arena for a media forum to promote another track's race. It was a most courteous gesture on the part of the Alabama track's staff to help take the sport of NASCAR Winston Cup racing to another level.

The event was, perhaps, the most publicized race in the history of the sport. Television stations in the Indianapolis market originated hour-long, prime-time programs every night during the week leading up to the race. ESPN produced a series of "Countdown to Indianapolis" programs that ran weekly prior to the race. The Indianapolis newspapers created special sections for the event — one such section was more than 60 pages in length! NASCARWorld, the traveling "theme park on wheels" dedicated to the sport, made its debut in downtown Indianapolis during the weekend.

The impact of the event was felt everywhere. In Phoenix, when ABC affiliate KTVK-TV announced it would air the tape-delayed Cardinals/49ers NFL football game followed by the Goodwill Games instead of the Brickyard 400, more than 1,000 angry

fans lit up the station's switchboard. Within hours, the station's management decided that the race would be shown live instead of the football/Goodwill Games combination! And at the Indy airport, preparations were underway to accommodate the 167 corporate jets which would land with passengers for the event. It would take more than five hours to clear out the private aircraft on Saturday afternoon!

When the gates finally opened, every driver in the field — more than 70 trying for the maximum 44 available spots — headed for the mandatory "rookie" meeting. Because it was the first event at a new track on the tour, every driver was considered a rookie!

Due to the number of entries and the time necessary to run a qualifying session, NASCAR officials made a slight change to the qualifying procedure in an attempt to make qualifying as equal as possible. In the draw for first-round qualifying positions, those who drew the "late" numbers and didn't make the field the first day would run early in the second session. Those who drew the "early" numbers would run late in the second session. The change would go into effect at every track, beginning at Indianapolis.

Texaco and Pennzoil used the event to announce extensions of their sponsorship agreements with Robert Yates Racing and Bahari Racing, respectively. Texaco bumped its deal to three more years, and Pennzoil backed Bahari for two more seasons. Also, rumors ran hot and heavy that Bill Elliott would turn the Dawsonville shop into a drive-through for a Big Mac and fries in 1995. It was rumored that McDonald's was leaving Junior Johnson and Jimmy Spencer to sponsor the new Elliott effort in 1995. Budweiser was also said to be leaving Junior as well; they appeared headed for Ken Schrader and the Hendrick Motorsports team.

Problems beset the Texaco team from the onset of practice: Irvan blew up the qualifying motor in the Havoline Ford during the first practice session, and then the race engine went sour during the second practice session. The team had gone through two motors before the first qualifying period Thursday afternoon!

Teams expected the track to be hot at the beginning of the pole-qualifying session, but heavy thunderstorms two hours prior to the session cooled the track down. Qualifying began, but as it progressed, the track heated up again from the sun.

Rick Mast took advantage of the situation. Mast, with Hoosier tires on his Skoal Classic Ford, was the 13th driver on the track. Dale Earnhardt had run just before Mast and had posted the fastest time so far, so Mast knew exactly what he had to beat. His lap was two-tenths of a second faster than Dale's — 172.414 miles per hour — but the Virginian then had to wait out the remainder of the 70 drivers who tried to make the field during the first day.

At qualifying's conclusion, Mast claimed the biggest

payday of his career. The pole earned him $50,000 in cash, a $40,000 van and a $10,000 bonus for Richard Jackson, his car owner, and the Skoal crew. Jeff Gordon claimed the inside of the second row ahead of Geoff Bodine. Bobby Labonte and Bill Elliott were right behind them in the third row. Brett Bodine and Ricky Rudd made up the fourth row, and Sterling Marlin and Mark Martin were the final drivers in the top 10. Point leader Irvan qualified 17th.

After pre-race festivities, marching bands and Jim Nabors' rousing rendition of the national anthem, Indianapolis matriarch Mary Fendrich Hulman gave the command for the drivers to start their engines. Finally, it was time to go.

Go, they did. Earnhardt, determined to lead the first lap, smacked the concrete wall on the exit of the fourth turn and damaged the toe-in on his right front tire. That slip removed him from contention to win the inaugural Brickyard 400, but he managed to manhandle the Chevrolet to a fifth-place finish. Mast maintained the point, but on the second lap, young Indiana native Gordon muscled his way past Mast to the lead. Geoff Bodine, proving his Hoosiers were up to the task, then moved to the front. During green-flag stops, seven other drivers led before the lead cycled back around to Gordon.

After the fourth caution, the field lined up with Brett Bodine in the lead and older brother Geoff immediately behind as the field rumbled under the green flag to start lap 100. Coming out of the third turn, Geoff and Brett made contact, and the Exide Ford spun right in front of the entire field. Dale Jarrett, with nowhere to go, collided with Geoff. Both were finished for the day.

The final caution of the race flew when Geoff Brabham and Jimmy Hensley got together on lap 131. The leaders hit pit road, and Rusty's team responded as it had all year, turning the Miller Ford back onto the track first. Gordon was second, ahead of Irvan, Brett, Elliott and Marlin.

Gordon immediately dispatched Wallace, and as Rusty went high and checked up to stay off the wall, Irvan slipped through to second place. Four laps later, Ernie was the 13th leader of the race — an Indianapolis record. Jeff again passed Ernie, but Irvan re-assumed the lead with 10 laps remaining.

Finally, with four laps remaining, Gordon moved to the inside of Irvan and made the pass for the lead. Simultaneously, the black Ford headed for the inside of the track, allowing a pack of cars to fly by. Irvan had fallen off the pace due to a flat right-front tire; after the stop to replace the tire, he staggered home to finish a lap in arrears.

Jeff streaked to the enormously popular victory. He had grown up just a few miles from the most famous track in the world and had come home to win the inaugural running of the Brickyard 400 by more than a half-second over Brett Bodine. Elliott was third, ahead of Wallace and Earnhardt, while Darrell Waltrip, Schrader, Michael Waltrip, Todd Bodine and Morgan Shepherd completed the top 10. A total of 16 cars finished on the lead lap!

After the last caution, Rusty Wallace's crew put him out in the lead, but the muscle under the hood of Jeff Gordon's Chevrolet was more than enough to handle both Wallace and Ernie Irvan.

The DuPont driver accepted both the PPG (!) trophy and the race trophy in victory lane. He hoisted the sterling silver brick aloft and reveled with his team after winning the race no one ever expected to take place. To be able to win the race at Indianapolis, just 15 minutes away from his former hometown of Pittsboro, and hear lusty cheers rising from 300,000 throats was nearly more than the fresh-faced youngster could bear!

Dave Marcis' new Chevrolet ended up on the hook after Marcis tangled with NASCAR Winston West Series leader Mike Chase.

Fin. Pos.	Str. Pos.	Car #	Driver	Team	Fin. Pos.	Str. Pos.	Car #	Driver	Team
1	3	24	Jeff Gordon	DuPont Chevrolet	23	22	43	Wally Dallenbach	STP Pontiac
2	7	26	Brett Bodine	Quaker State Ford	24	32	40	Bobby Hamilton	Kendall Pontiac
3	6	11	Bill Elliott	Budweiser Ford	25	36	42	Kyle Petty	Mello Yello Pontiac
4	12	2	Rusty Wallace	Miller Genuine Draft Ford	26	31	98	Jeremy Mayfield	Fingerhut Ford
5	2	3	Dale Earnhardt	GM Goodwrench Chevrolet	27	39	02	Derrike Cope	Children's Miracle Network Ford
6	27	17	Darrell Waltrip	Western Auto Chevrolet	28	28	14	John Andretti	Bryant Chevrolet
7	23	25	Ken Schrader	Kodiak Chevrolet	29	19	9	Rich Bickle	Orkin Pest Control Ford
8	15	30	Michael Waltrip	Pennzoil Pontiac	30	40	50	A.J. Foyt	Copenhagen Ford
9	25	75	Todd Bodine	Factory Stores of America Ford	31	33	31	Ward Burton	Hardee's Chevrolet
10	11	21	Morgan Shepherd	Citgo Ford	32	24	55	Jimmy Hensley	Bondo/Mar-Hyde Ford
11	8	10	Ricky Rudd	Tide Ford	33	26	99	Danny Sullivan	Corporate Car Chevrolet
12	21	5	Terry Labonte	Kellogg's Corn Flakes Chevrolet	34	29	51	Jeff Purvis	Country Time Chevrolet
13	37	16	Ted Musgrave	The Family Channel Ford	35	10	6	Mark Martin	Valvoline Ford
14	9	4	Sterling Marlin	Kodak Film Chevrolet	36	20	23	Hut Stricklin	Smokin' Joe's Ford
15	41	15	Lake Speed	Quality Care Ford	37	42	33	Harry Gant	Skoal Bandit Chevrolet
16	5	22	Bobby Labonte	Maxwell House Coffee Pontiac	38	18	07	Geoff Brabham	K-Mart Ford
17	17	28	Ernie Irvan	Texaco Havoline Ford	39	4	7	Geoff Bodine	Exide Batteries Ford
18	13	77	Greg Sacks	USAir Ford	40	14	18	Dale Jarrett	Interstate Batteries Chevrolet
19	38	8	Jeff Burton	Raybestos Brakes Ford	41	16	71	Dave Marcis	Terramite Const. Equip. Chevrolet
20	30	41	Joe Nemechek	Meineke Mufflers Chevrolet	42	43	58	Mike Chase	Tyson Foods Chevrolet
21	35	44	Bobby Hillin	Buss Fuses Ford	43	34	27	Jimmy Spencer	McDonald's Ford
22	1	1	Rick Mast	Skoal Classic Ford					

THE BUD AT THE GLEN

Despite losing a chance to win the Brickyard 400 (due to a first-lap scrape with the concrete retaining wall), Dale Earnhardt was able to use his fifth-place finish and Ernie Irvan's late-race flat tire to vault back into the lead in the NASCAR Winston Cup point standings. Now, the teams were rolling into the lush road course at Watkins Glen, NY, for the Budweiser at The Glen.

(Top) After starting 21st, Lake Speed took Bud Moore's Thunderbird to the lead before finishing 13th in The Budweiser at The Glen. (Right) Car owner Jack Roush and driver Mark Martin celebrate their first victory of the season, the result of a dominant performance by Martin and the Valvoline Ford.

The Glen's management team and the communities surrounding the track once again outdid themselves with regard to community support for the NASCAR Winston Cup race. More than 35,000 turned out for the headline event, "Race Fever" night, in Corning, just 14 miles from the track.

There were plenty of things to do in the region — from visiting the state parks to touring the area wineries — and as spectators enjoyed the days leading to the annual outing on the winding 2.4-mile track, events surrounding the race grabbed the headlines time and again.

Billy Hagan said his team would cut back its schedule drastically due to its inability to find a sponsor. John Andretti became a free agent. Richard Petty announced that the Glen event would be the last time Wally Dallenbach would suit up in STP livery. Petty later said that Andretti would drive the Pontiac at Michigan in a "trial" run.

Lake Speed told Bud Moore he would not return in 1995 as the pilot of the Quality Care Fords.

Dale Jarrett qualified his Interstate Batteries Chevrolet 14th and powered to an 11th-place finish at The Glen.

Sabates' Kendall Oil Pontiac, driven by Bobby Hamilton. On a somber note, word reached The Glen Saturday afternoon that Frank Wilson, the popular president and CEO of North Carolina Motor Speedway, had suffered a stroke and was hospitalized in South Carolina.

With all this going on, Brickyard winner Jeff Gordon quickly found himself yanked back from Fantasyland! After winning the previous week, he had been on a whirlwind tour of DisneyWorld, where he was the parade's grand marshal. But now, just a few hours after zipping down Space Mountain, reality had set in. It was time to belt back into a race car.

At the start of The Glen, Ernie was 27 points behind leader Dale Earnhardt, and Rusty Wallace had moved

Derrike Cope signed on with Bobby Allison's team, and Straight Arrow Products, Inc. announced it would sponsor Allison's Ford effort at The Glen. Allison hoped

Rusty Wallace ran with the lead pack all day, but a mistake at the end of the race cost him mightily.

to persuade the equine shampoo-maker to extend its sponsorship through the remainder of the season.

Spencer was unable to race at The Glen, and Junior Johnson nominated Tommy Kendall to drive the McDonald's Ford. Former driver Dick Brooks, now a successful businessman and part-time MRN Radio commentator, was named the new co-owner of Felix

back to third in the standings, 268 in arrears. Mark Martin's motor problem at Indianapolis had left him fourth, now 344 behind. There were no tomorrows for Martin and the Valvoline team as far as the championship was concerned.

But The Glen had been the catalyst for Martin's four-race winning streak last year, and Mark was determined

In a position to capitalize on his opponents' mistakes late in the race, Dale Earnhardt did just that, moving up to a third-place finish in the closing laps.

to get things rolling again. And during the first round of qualifying, Mark took his first step towards defending the Budweiser at The Glen championship he won last year: He notched his first pole of the season, beating Kenny Schrader by less than a tenth of a second around the serpentine track.

Gordon may have learned something while rocketing through the right and left turns at Space Mountain. He was the third-fastest qualifier, ahead of Irvan and Wallace. But Earnhardt was not about to let his challengers get out of sight. He turned the sixth-fastest lap, ahead of Ricky Rudd, a resurgent Bill Elliott and Dallenbach, who posted a fine ninth place in his last outing for Petty Enterprises. Terry Labonte completed the top 10, just nipping Morgan Shepherd for the last spot. Cope gave Allison and the new sponsorship reason to cheer, qualifying 17th.

(Below) Ernie Irvan never led the race, but he ran strongly enough to finish second behind a dominant Mark Martin.

Rain washed out the second round of qualifying, forcing Rick Mast and Greg Sacks to take provisionals. Scott Gaylord, Loy Allen, Jeremy Mayfield, Mike Wallace and Brian Bonner were sent home for the remainder of the weekend.

Once the race began, Martin wasted no time demonstrating that his Valvoline Ford would be as good racing as it had been in qualifying. In a display of complete domination, Mark motored away from the field and led 75 of the 90 laps.

The outcome was only in doubt once — a late caution triggered by Hut Stricklin's spin in the last turn set up a five-lap sprint to the checkered flag. But with 17 cars on the lead lap, no one pitted for fear of giving up track position. The only car able to stay within hailing distance of Mark throughout the race had been Irvan, and the black Ford was right behind the red, white and blue Valvoline machine on the restart.

But Mark had no problem with Irvan and eased to a .88-second victory. But a battle raged behind those two.

Dallenbach tried to pass Wallace for third, but slid wide in the final turn. A lap later, Wallace over-cooked it into the next-to-last turn, slid on the grass and came back onto the course, clipping Wally and damaging both cars. Wally slid wide again on the final turn with one lap to go. In the end, Dallenbach fell to 14th and Wallace struggled around to finish 17th — the final car on the lead lap.

With Wallace and Dallenbach shucking and jiving in front of him, Earnhardt played the waiting game and then took over third place when the two dropped back through the field. Schrader was fourth and Rudd fifth. Terry Labonte came home sixth ahead of Darrell Waltrip, Joe Nemechek, Gordon and Harry Gant.

Because Earnhardt had led a lap and Irvan hadn't, the point gap between the two remained the same at the top of the standings. Martin, having led the most laps, gained 15 points but still trailed by 329. Wallace suffered the biggest point drop, losing 58 points. Rusty was now 326 behind, and just 11 races remained on the schedule.

Rusty Wallace over-cooked it and got into the grass, which cost him positions in the final laps of the race at The Glen.

Mark Martin's .88-of-a-second victory was no indication of how strongly he ran at The Glen. A caution turned the race into a six-lap sprint at the end, and Mark simply motored away from Ernie Irvan.

Fin. Pos.	Str. Pos.	Car #	Driver	Team	Fin. Pos.	Str. Pos.	Car #	Driver	Team
1	1	6	Mark Martin	Valvoline Ford	21	34	71	Dave Marcis	Mr. Salt Chevrolet
2	4	28	Ernie Irvan	Texaco Havoline Ford	22	27	27	Tom Kendall	McDonald's Ford
3	6	3	Dale Earnhardt	GM Goodwrench Chevrolet	23	32	29	Steve Grissom	Diamond Ridge Chevrolet
4	2	25	Ken Schrader	Kodiak Chevrolet	24	30	31	Ward Burton	Hardee's Chevrolet
5	7	10	Ricky Rudd	Tide Ford	25	36	8	Jeff Burton	Raybestos Brakes Ford
6	10	5	Terry Labonte	Kellogg's Corn Flakes Chevrolet	26	22	4	Sterling Marlin	Kodak Film Chevrolet
7	13	17	Darrell Waltrip	Western Auto Chevrolet	27	28	34	Mike McLaughlin	Coors Chevrolet
8	23	41	Joe Nemechek	Meineke Mufflers Chevrolet	28	16	26	Brett Bodine	Quaker State Ford
9	3	24	Jeff Gordon	DuPont Chevrolet	29	15	7	Geoff Bodine	Exide Batteries Ford
10	25	33	Harry Gant	Skoal Bandit Chevrolet	30	18	23	Hut Stricklin	Smokin' Joe's Ford
11	14	18	Dale Jarrett	Interstate Batteries Chevrolet	31	38	03	Butch Leitzinger	McIntosh Equipment Chevrolet
12	8	11	Bill Elliott	Budweiser Ford	32	33	32	Dick Trickle	Active Trucking Chevrolet
13	21	15	Lake Speed	Quality Care Ford	33	37	55	Jimmy Hensley	RaDiUs Motorsports Ford
14	9	43	Wally Dallenbach	STP Pontiac	34	31	40	Bobby Hamilton	Kendall Pontiac
15	24	75	Todd Bodine	Factory Stores of America Ford	35	35	88	P.J. Jones	Tops Friendly Markets Ford
16	11	21	Morgan Shepherd	Citgo Ford	36	26	39	Scott Lagasse	Pedigree Chevrolet
17	5	2	Rusty Wallace	Miller Genuine Draft Ford	37	20	42	Kyle Petty	Mello Yello Pontiac
18	12	22	Bobby Labonte	Maxwell House Coffee Pontiac	38	39	1	Rick Mast	Skoal Classic Ford
19	29	16	Ted Musgrave	The Family Channel Ford	39	40	77	Greg Sacks	USAir Ford
20	19	30	Michael Waltrip	Pennzoil Pontiac	40	17	12	Derrike Cope	Straight Arrow Ford

GM GOODWRENCH DEALER 400

MICHIGAN
INTERNATIONAL SPEEDWAY

AUGUST 21, 1994

Normally, the August weekend at Michigan is one of the most pleasant of the season. The back-roads drive to the race track from Ann Arbor is a tour of small lakes and pastoral farms, and fresh roasted corn is always a feature in one corner of the garage area at Roger Penske's ultra-friendly two-miler.

This time, though, the NASCAR Winston Cup tour's trip to the Irish Hills of Michigan had more on its agenda than a sampling of Michigan corn!

Phil Parsons had replaced Rich Bickle as the driver of Harry Melling's Ford, and both Phil and Harry hoped to do well at MIS. Phil is a native of the nearby Detroit area, and Melling's company is headquartered in Jackson, less than 30 minutes from the track.

Jimmy Spencer, after a weekend off at The Glen, returned to the cockpit of the McDonald's Ford. Les Richter, NASCAR's vice president for competition, was not present at The Glen; it was the first race the affable NASCAR official had missed in years. Richter was busy at work on the new California Speedway, which would be built near the old Ontario

(Top) Darrell Waltrip (17), Ricky Rudd (10) and Ken Schrader battle for ninth position. They would finish in this same order: Waltrip captured ninth, Rudd 10th and Schrader 11th. (Right) Michigan marked John Andretti's debut in Richard Petty's STP Pontiac. John raised more than a few eyebrows when he qualified for the outside of the front row.

Rusty Wallace and Bill Elliott (11) race side by side on the "D" oval with Terry Labonte in hot pursuit. Rusty went on to finish in fourth place; Elliott and Labonte wound up seventh and eighth – one lap down.

location. Former Atlanta and Talladega general manager Mike Helton is now capably in charge of competition.

NASCAR's members traditionally have participated in fund-raising and charitable activities, and on the Thursday evening before the start of practice, a total of 16 Winston Cup and Busch Grand National drivers participated in a dinner and auction to raise money for a local Michigan Boy Scout council. The dinner honored NASCAR President Bill France Jr. By the end of the evening, more than $100,000 was raised for the Scouts!

The Family Channel announced it would extend its sponsorship program with the Jack Roush team. Kendall Oil said it would step up for another year as sponsor of the second Felix Sabates team, which is now co-owned by Dick Brooks. And Bobby Allison Motorsports, with new partner Ron Zook on board, made the announcement that Straight Arrow Products, the sponsor of their car at The Glen, would extend its program for the remainder of this year, all of '95 and all of '96. Derrike Cope would drive the Ford for the remainder of the season. The team also introduced its new blue, red and yellow paint scheme.

By the conclusion of the first qualifying session for what teams call the "Backyard 400" (because of its proximity to the Ford and General Motors headquarters and the executives who make the racing decisions!),

Darrell Waltrip and Dave Marcis are longtime veterans of the Winston Cup wars. Prior to the 1994 season, their two records combined add up to more than 1,300 starts and 48 seasons behind the wheel!

Geoff Bodine had claimed bragging rights for the Blue Oval bunch.

Geoff Bodine, driving the car he used at Indy, took advantage of his Hoosiers to streak to his third pole of the season. But the biggest news of the day was that John Andretti, wearing a hastily-made driver's suit (which was at least two sizes too large for his frame), just missed unseating Bodine for the pole in his first outing in the STP Pontiac. John was only nine-thousandths of a

second behind Bodine and nearly won the pole for Petty Enterprises — it would've been their first since 1979! It was the first time a Petty Enterprises entry had worn a yellow (rookie) bumper stripe since 1953!

Behind Geoff and John were Jeff Gordon and a surging Bill Elliott, comfortable on one of his favorite race tracks. Bobby Labonte and Joe Nemechek made up the third row. Rusty Wallace was inside the fourth row alongside Todd Bodine. Rick Mast and Michael Waltrip completed the top 10, just ahead of point leader Dale Earnhardt. Mark Martin qualified 13th, while Ernie Irvan, trailing Earnhardt in the point chase by just 27, suffered through an atypical session and qualified only 19th fastest.

Dale Jarrett's team was without its crew chief during the first qualifying session. Jimmy Makar was home in North Carolina where his wife, Patti (who is Jarrett's sister), gave birth to twins! Crew members tried to figure out whether to build the stroller body with the driver's and navigator's seats in-line or side by side!

Kyle Petty and Jimmy Spencer took the provisional positions. Bobby Hamilton, Hut Stricklin, Jimmy Hensley, Robert Pressley, Andy Belmont, Laura Lane, Brad Teague and Bob Brevak all loaded up and went home after failing to make the field.

During the first practice session Saturday morning, Ernie Irvan cut a right-front tire and crashed in the first turn while completing a 10-lap run. He was competently extracted from the Havoline Ford and air-lifted by medical helicopter to an Ann Arbor hospital with serious injuries, and both his teams withdrew their entries for the weekend.

Sunday, as teams prepared for the race, word of the death of North Carolina Motor Speedway's Frank Wilson reached the speedway. Wilson had suffered a stroke the previous weekend while vacationing in South Carolina and suffered another during the week. The genial president and CEO of Rockingham's one-mile track died Saturday night. Like Darlington's Red Tyler, who died earlier in the season, Wilson was one of the best-liked track officials on the tour, and the entire NASCAR family mourned the loss of the track executive.

Although the mood was somber, teams continued with the business of the race at hand. Mark Martin had administered an old-fashioned whipping the previous week at Watkins Glen, but when the flag dropped on the Goodwrench Dealer 400, it quickly became obvious that

Geoff Bodine looks dominant in victory lane. He should: Geoff qualified the Exide Ford on the pole and led 80 percent of the laps on the way to his second win of the season.

Jack Roush and his second-year driver, Ted Musgrave, shared their good news during the weekend at Michigan: The Family Channel had agreed to extend its sponsorship of the Roush Racing Ford.

more than 13 seconds on the way to his second victory of the season.

Earnhardt, whose 300-plus point lead over Wallace and Martin seemed unassailable after Irvan's wreck removed him from the championship picture, found himself in the middle of a track-side tangle just past quarter-distance. Todd Bodine and Earnhardt got into it, and Dale crashed into the concrete wall. Earnhardt hurriedly left the track, but his team was unable to affect repairs. It was the first time Earnhardt was unable to finish a race due to wreck damage since 1986!

Martin and Wallace took advantage of the situation. With Bodine so far ahead, only late-race cautions enabled the others to close the distance on the black and blue Ford. Wallace, however, had uncharacteristic problems in his

it was Geoff Bodine's turn. The Exide Ford driver led early — and often — and ran off with a seven-car-length victory over Martin. Bodine led four times for 159 of the 200 laps comprising the race, and, at times, built leads of

pits. The Miller Ford ran out of gas, stalled on pit road, fell off its jack and received mismatched tire sets — the list seemed endless. Despite the problems, Wallace managed to finish fourth and gain points on Earnhardt.

Michigan International Speedway is well-known for accommodating multiple racing grooves. Here, drivers make it four-wide on the frontstretch – a common site at MIS.

146

Rick Mast matched his best finish of the season by coming home third behind Martin. Bobby Labonte had the highest-finishing Pontiac, and Kyle Petty came from 40th place to finish sixth. Bill Elliott and Darrell Waltrip kept their hot streaks alive with seventh and ninth place finishes. A pair of brothers graced the top eight when Terry Labonte finished eighth. Ricky Rudd claimed the final position in the top 10.

Earnhardt was classified 37th.

While the points were being tallied, teams loaded up for the long drive south. The "Backyard 400" was over, and a Ford had won the GM Goodwrench Dealer 400. General Motors teams would have to wait until next June to try to win in their home state.

Crew chief Barry Dodson (on left) lends a hand as crew members push the Mello Yello Pontiac to the line before qualifying. Driver Kyle Petty did not qualify well; he was forced to use a provisional and started from the 40th position.

Fin. Pos.	Str. Pos.	Car #	Driver	Team	Fin. Pos.	Str. Pos.	Car #	Driver	Team
1	1	7	Geoff Bodine	Exide Batteries Ford	22	14	19	Loy Allen	Hooters Ford
2	13	6	Mark Martin	Valvoline Ford	23	39	98	Jeremy Mayfield	Fingerhut Ford
3	9	1	Rick Mast	Skoal Classic Ford	24	38	16	Ted Musgrave	The Family Channel Ford
4	7	2	Rusty Wallace	Miller Genuine Draft Ford	25	18	33	Harry Gant	Skoal Bandit Chevrolet
5	5	22	Bobby Labonte	Maxwell House Coffee Pontiac	26	36	21	Morgan Shepherd	Citgo Ford
6	40	42	Kyle Petty	Mello Yello Pontiac	27	35	61	Rick Carelli	Total Petroleum Chevrolet
7	4	11	Bill Elliott	Budweiser Ford	28	23	02	Jeff Purvis	Children's Miracle Network Ford
8	17	5	Terry Labonte	Kellogg's Corn Flakes Chevrolet	29	26	31	Ward Burton	Hardee's Chevrolet
9	30	17	Darrell Waltrip	Western Auto Chevrolet	30	31	18	Dale Jarrett	Interstate Batteries Chevrolet
10	15	10	Ricky Rudd	Tide Ford	31	33	9	Phil Parsons	Farmer Peet Ford
11	19	25	Ken Schrader	Kodiak Chevrolet	32	16	77	Greg Sacks	USAir Ford
12	21	26	Brett Bodine	Quaker State Ford	33	28	8	Jeff Burton	Raybestos Brakes Ford
13	29	15	Lake Speed	Quality Care Ford	34	12	4	Sterling Marlin	Kodak Film Chevrolet
14	10	30	Michael Waltrip	Pennzoil Pontiac	35	22	45	Rich Bickle	Terminal Trucking Ford
15	3	24	Jeff Gordon	DuPont Chevrolet	36	37	71	Dave Marcis	Prodigy/Terramite Chevrolet
16	27	90	Mike Wallace	Heilig-Meyers Ford	37	11	3	Dale Earnhardt	GM Goodwrench Chevrolet
17	2	43	John Andretti	STP Pontiac	38	8	75	Todd Bodine	Factory Stores of America Ford
18	24	12	Derrike Cope	Straight Arrow Ford	39	25	47	Billy Standridge	Standridge Auto Parts Ford
19	20	29	Steve Grissom	Diamond Ridge Chevrolet	40	32	44	Bobby Hillin	Buss Fuses Ford
20	41	27	Jimmy Spencer	McDonald's Ford	41	34	32	Dick Trickle	Active Trucking Chevrolet
21	6	41	Joe Nemechek	Meineke Mufflers Chevrolet					

GOODY'S 500

Heartened by news of Ernie Irvan's improvement, the NASCAR Winston Cup competitors unloaded at Larry Carrier's speed bowl in Thunder Valley to do battle under the arc-lights in the annual "Saturday Night Special." A huge crowd, guaranteed by the race's sold-out grandstands, saw Dale Earnhardt in the point lead, Ricky Rudd as a first-time father, Rusty Wallace sporting new colors on his driver's suit, Kenny Wallace behind the wheel of the "28" and former champions Bill Elliott and Darrell Waltrip in the middle of hot streaks.

(Top) Harry Gant and his team worked hard all night in an attempt to capture his first win of the season, but he could only manage eighth. (Right) Rusty Wallace gets a kiss from his wife, Patty, after his sixth victory of the season. It was his first outing in his new gold driver's suit.

Aided by the combination of Earnhardt's wreck at Michigan and their own top five finishes, Mark Martin and Rusty had closed the gap somewhat on Dale's point lead. But both Wallace and Martin knew that if they were to have a chance at the title, they needed to run in the top three for the remainder of the season and hope that Earnhardt was struck with bad luck at least one more time. If Dale continued to run in the top five, as he had throughout most of the

UNOCAL 76
Miller Genuine Draft
Mobil 1
GOODYEAR
STEVENS AVIATION
Ford
BOSCH
Miller
94 GOODY'S 50
76

season, he would pose an insurmountable obstacle for the two contenders.

But Wallace couldn't have been happier. He was back at the short tracks where his record over the previous season-and-a-half of competition was unsurpassed. He was also wearing a gold driver's suit with black trim, instead of the black suit he had worn for nearly two years. Team owner Roger Penske had suggested the change, telling Wallace it would change his luck. Rusty was willing to try just about anything if it would help him catch Earnhardt!

Martin, with a win and a second place in his last two outings, felt his Valvoline Ford was the car to beat. He now trailed Earnhardt by only 206 points, although Wallace

Harry Gant scored a clean sweep of the pole positions at Bristol. He won the Busch pole for the Winston Cup race and also won the pole for the Friday night Busch Grand National series race.

was a mere seven points behind him. Beginning with the Bristol race, 10 races remained on the schedule, so there was still time to make a charge toward the title.

No one in the field, however, was prepared for what Harry Gant had up the sleeves of his driver's suit for the Busch and Winston Cup qualifying sessions!

Gant had struggled in his final season. His best opportunity to win had been at Pocono: He had been cruising behind Geoff Bodine with a 13-second cushion over the rest of the field when an oil fitting broke. He had entered the season with goals of winning poles in NASCAR Busch Series and NASCAR Winston Cup events, as well as posting wins in both series. Gant was determined to prove that at age 54, he still had the juice to beat all those young whippersnappers.

By the end of qualifying, Gant was three-quarters of the way to his goal. In addition to his Atlanta Busch win in March, Harry turned

Joe Nemechek and Jeff Gordon do battle. Gordon finished second while Nemechek and the Meineke Chevrolet finished 29th.

Dale Earnhardt won the battle with Kenny Wallace, who was driving
for Ernie Irvan in the Havoline Ford. Earnhardt finished third, behind
Rusty Wallace and Mark Martin. Kenny finished 13th, a lap down.

the fastest qualifying laps for both the NASCAR Busch
series and NASCAR Winston Cup races at Bristol. If the
Taylorsville driver had grinned any wider, he would have
cracked his face!

Geoff Bodine completed an all-Hoosier front row,
turning his lap just .01 of a second slower than Gant.
Terry Labonte and Rusty, the best Goodyear qualifiers,
were in the second row, and Joe Nemechek continued his
strong qualifying efforts with the fifth-fastest lap, just
ahead of a hot-running Dick Trickle. Ward Burton and
Mark Martin made up the fourth row, with Rick Mast
and Bobby Labonte completing the top 10. Elliott, who
had put together three top seven finishes in his last four
races to climb from 18th to 11th in the standings, was
11th, while Darrell, with three straight top nine finishes,

qualified 16th. Earnhardt would start 14th, with Kenny
Wallace, subbing for Irvan, alongside him.

Rudd received a phone call at 3:10 p.m. Friday and was
instructed to head over the mountain to Winston Salem.
His wife, Linda, had gone into labor with their first
child. Ricky turned his car over to Larry Pearson for

John Andretti and STP Pontiac crew chief Robbie Loomis thought
they had something going, but John finished 30th after
he was involved in a wreck.

Geoff Bodine stands in front of a fan to study his competition's lap times before making his own qualifying run. Geoff must have found what he was looking for; he qualified second fastest, right behind Harry Gant.

season and his second in a row. But his water pump failed in the final 100 laps. Meanwhile, Rusty Wallace's crew members were able to redeem themselves after the previous week's problems on pit road. Three times in the final 200 laps, the Miller team got Wallace off pit road and into the lead, including a critical final yellow-flag stop with less than 40 laps to go. Bodine had retired with a burned piston, so the final sprint to victory included Wallace, Earnhardt, Martin, Gant and Darrell Waltrip. Waltrip had played the waiting game and was now in a position to run for the win.

Martin put Earnhardt away, set out after Wallace and had Rusty in his sights with five laps to go. But lapped traffic came into play, and Mark couldn't get close enough. Rusty's margin was just over two car-lengths. Behind them, Gant tried every possible part of the track — including the apron — to get past Earnhardt. But Harry burned his Hoosiers to the ground in his

qualifying, waved a hurried "bye" to his team and headed for the airport.

The proud father returned Saturday after the birth of his son and made it into the field after the second round of qualifying. Lake Speed took his second provisional of the season and Todd Bodine used one after wrecking his primary car in first-round qualifying. Jeff Green, Jimmy Spencer, Dave Marcis, Loy Allen, Jimmy Hensley and Phil Parsons failed to make the field. Parsons was driving Billy Hagan's Chevrolet. Hut Stricklin was told by car owner Travis Carter that the team would go with a new driver next season. Hut, in the meantime, put the Camel Ford into the field at Bristol with the 26th-fastest lap.

From the start of the newly named Goody's 500, it appeared that Gant and his Skoal team finally had figured out the chassis settings which had eluded them all season. The green and white Chevrolet established itself at the front of the field, and for the first 88 laps, looked like the car to beat. Despite slipping back slightly, Harry ran with the leaders until the final 100 laps.

When Gant fell back, Geoff took the Exide Ford to the point and looked ready to win his third race of the

Kenny Wallace, in his first outing behind the wheel of the Havoline Ford, and crew chief Larry McReynolds keep an eye on the competition. Kenny substituted for Ernie Irvan following Ernie's accident at Michigan.

efforts to pass the Goodwrench driver and was forced to pit for new rubber with 14 laps left. His promising run ended in ninth place.

Behind Earnhardt came Darrell with his fourth-straight top-10. Bill Elliott was right on his tail for fifth place, which moved him to 10th in the point standings. Sterling Marlin and Michael Waltrip were sixth and seventh, and Todd Bodine had the final car on the lead lap. Mast claimed the final top-10 position right behind Skoal teammate Gant.

Mark Martin tries to hold off Brad Teague and a hard-charging Dale Earnhardt.

Fin. Pos.	Str. Pos.	Car #	Driver	Team	Fin. Pos.	Str. Pos.	Car #	Driver	Team
1	4	2	Rusty Wallace	Miller Genuine Draft Ford	19	31	25	Ken Schrader	Kodiak Chevrolet
2	8	6	Mark Martin	Valvoline Ford	20	20	8	Jeff Burton	Raybestos Brakes Ford
3	14	3	Dale Earnhardt	GM Goodwrench Chevrolet	21	25	98	Jeremy Mayfield	Fingerhut Ford
4	16	17	Darrell Waltrip	Western Auto Chevrolet	22	34	52	Brad Teague	NAPA Ford
5	11	11	Bill Elliott	Budweiser Ford	23	2	7	Geoff Bodine	Exide Batteries Ford
6	24	4	Sterling Marlin	Kodak Film Chevrolet	24	27	90	Mike Wallace	Heilig-Meyers Ford
7	28	30	Michael Waltrip	Pennzoil Pontiac	25	35	15	Lake Speed	Quality Care Ford
8	36	75	Todd Bodine	Factory Stores of America Ford	26	29	18	Dale Jarrett	Interstate Batteries Chevrolet
9	1	33	Harry Gant	Skoal Bandit Chevrolet	27	13	77	Greg Sacks	USAir Ford
10	9	1	Rick Mast	Skoal Classic Ford	28	17	40	Bobby Hamilton	Kendall Pontiac
11	18	16	Ted Musgrave	The Family Channel Ford	29	5	41	Joe Nemechek	Meineke Mufflers Chevrolet
12	33	10	Ricky Rudd	Tide Ford	30	23	43	John Andretti	STP Pontiac
13	15	28	Kenny Wallace	Texaco Havoline Ford	31	10	22	Bobby Labonte	Maxwell House Coffee Pontiac
14	22	26	Brett Bodine	Quaker State Ford	32	12	24	Jeff Gordon	DuPont Chevrolet
15	32	42	Kyle Petty	Mello Yello Pontiac	33	3	5	Terry Labonte	Kellogg's Corn Flakes Chevrolet
16	19	12	Derrike Cope	Straight Arrow Ford	34	30	29	Steve Grissom	Diamond Ridge Chevrolet
17	6	32	Dick Trickle	Active Trucking Chevrolet	35	26	23	Hut Stricklin	Smokin' Joe's Ford
18	21	21	Morgan Shepherd	Citgo Ford	36	7	31	Ward Burton	Hardee's Chevrolet

MOUNTAIN DEW SOUTHERN 500

DARLINGTON RACEWAY   SEPTEMBER 4, 1994

Above all things, Dale Earnhardt is a racer. There is nothing he dislikes more than being unable to do everything in his power to put his car in victory lane. After 62 victories and six championships, Earnhardt may have mellowed a bit from his attitude of the early '80s, but the fire to win every Sunday still burns hotly within him.

So, with a 200-plus point lead, Earnhardt wanted nothing to do with conservative running or "stroking" toward a record-tying seventh title. If

(Top) Geoff Bodine (on the inside) and Kenny Schrader (on the outside) lead the field under the green flag to start the Mountain Dew Southern 500. (Right) Bill Elliott won his third career Southern 500 despite an overheating Budweiser Ford; it held on just long enough to snap his long winless string.

"stroking" was to occur, it wouldn't be at Darlington. In Earnhardt's estimation, there were simply too many events remaining in the season, and the best way to maintain the point lead was to race every event. High finishes produced points, and high finishes would maintain the lead over his closest competitors, Mark Martin (down 206) and Rusty Wallace (213 behind).

There was another reason Earnhardt was so set against running in a conservative fashion. This was Darlington. More importantly, this was the Mountain Dew Southern 500.

For some of the newer drivers in the sport, the Southern 500 may seem like just another event on the 31-race NASCAR Winston Cup tour.

But to drivers like Earnhardt, Harry Gant, Darrell Waltrip, Bill Elliott and others, this 500-mile test is one of most important races of the year. It is a supreme test of driving skill and car preparation. The Southern 500 tests the mettle of the engine builder, crew chief and crew members — most of all, it is a measuring stick used to determine the success or failure of a driver's career. To beat old Darlington in the sweat and grime of Labor Day weekend is one of the sweetest victories to be had in a lifetime of sliding through race car windows.

Only nine drivers in the 44-year history of the race have been able to win the Southern 500 more than once. Earnhardt, Elliott and Gant are three of them, and all three keep their Southern 500 trophies in special places in their trophy rooms.

The fact that this was the final round for the Winston Select Million program — Earnhardt, along with Jeff Gordon and Sterling Marlin, were eligible for the $100,000 Winston "consolation" bonus if any of them could win the race — merely added incentive for Earnhardt and his Goodwrench team.

The September Darlington race is also the traditional induction site for new members of the National Motorsports Hall of Fame, and this year's ceremony was filled with Darlington history. The lone inductee this year was three-time Winston Cup champion Cale

Dale Earnhardt's crew worked solidly all day and kept Dale in the hunt for the win. Earnhardt gave up the lead to Bill Elliott with 12 laps remaining.

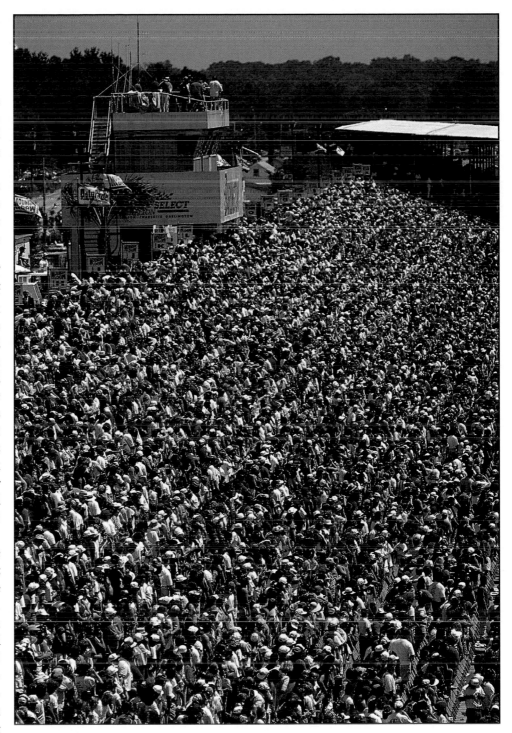

A sea of fans turned out to watch their favorites compete in the Mountain Dew Southern 500.

Yarborough, who started his racing career just yards away from the induction site when he raced a soap-box derby car down the adjacent hill.

No one is more familiar with the vagaries of Darlington's pavement than Cale. He is the only five-time winner of the Southern 500!

After a rain shower cooled off the track before the first round of qualifying, Geoff Bodine took advantage of every facet of his Ford, especially its engine and Hoosier tires, to claim his fourth pole of the season. His lap speed of nearly 167 mph shattered the lap record at Darlington but was barely enough to beat a banzai run by Kenny Schrader. Rookies Ward Burton and Joe Nemechek took the second row with their Hoosier-shod Chevrolets, and Brett Bodine and Martin claimed the third row on Goodyears.

Gordon and Bobby Labonte made up the fourth row. Elliott and Rick Mast would begin side by side in the final top 10 slots. Rusty and Earnhardt struggled in qualifying, turning the 19th- and 27th-fastest times. Rain washed out the second round of qualifying, so Loy Allen claimed a provisional. The second went to Butch Miller in the RaDiUs Racing Ford. (Jimmy Hensley, the team's regular driver, had been released after he failed to qualify at Bristol, and Miller was named to drive at Darlington.) Rick Carelli and Bob Schacht were unable to make the field.

Darlington's coarse surface ground the compound off the tires — Hoosiers lasted about 30 laps, and Goodyears about 10 more. This development threw yet another variable into crew chiefs' strategies regarding the prestigious old race. Also, the rubber coming off quickly deteriorating tires settled on radiator screens, necessitating thorough scrubbings on pit road to remove the rubble before it caused engines to overheat.

Schrader, trying to win after 99 consecutive losses, led early and often but fell victim to an oil leak with less than 100 laps to go. Earnhardt then moved to the point but gave it up to Martin with 60 laps to go. Then Mark fell out with engine failure with 25 laps remaining. Earnhardt moved back into the lead but began to lose the handle on his Chevrolet due to a "loose" set of tires.

Earnhardt, with a three-second lead, looked in the mirror and saw a red Ford beginning to close in on him. Despite an overheating motor, with water and oil temperatures running around 270 degrees, Bill Elliott decided to "go or blow" to bring an end to a winless

Brett Bodine spins as Geoff Bodine looks to keep away from trouble. Brett was able to continue and finished 29th.

streak that had lasted over a year-and-a-half. The Redhead nibbled, gnawed, chipped and chopped at the lead — a car-length here, a half-second there. With 12 laps to go, the Bud Ford swept past the Chevrolet.

Elliott pulled away to a six-second victory, but he had driven his Ford beyond the breaking point. The clutch was gone, and he could not get the car into reverse to get to the winner's circle. By the time the photographers had finished, a pool of oil more than two feet wide had spread under the Ford.

But Elliott had won for the first time since November of 1992 at Atlanta. Morgan Shepherd finished behind Earnhardt; Ricky Rudd and Marlin finished fourth and fifth. Gordon was sixth, and Rusty came home seventh after mistakes on pit road again cost him a chance to win. Jeff Burton, Dale Jarrett and Terry Labonte completed the top 10.

In victory lane, Elliott shared a congratulatory hug with Mike Beam, his teary-eyed crew chief. Beam (who, as a teenager, worked as a crew chief for Butch Lindley and later for Harry Gant in the NASCAR Sportsman ranks before moving up to Cup) had dreamed since childhood that he would one day win what he considered the most difficult race in NASCAR Winston Cup racing. Elliott's victory had brought Beam to the Southern 500 winner's circle. Beam's emotions were written all over his face.

Drivers aren't the only ones who understand the importance of winning this pioneer event.

Pit road is packed as drivers and crews work to get that split-second advantage.

Todd Bodine is hounded by a host of adversaries, including Michael Waltrip, Terry Labonte and Dale Earnhardt.

Fin. Pos.	Str. Pos.	Car #	Driver	Team	Fin. Pos.	Str. Pos.	Car #	Driver	Team
1	9	11	Bill Elliott	Budweiser Ford	22	16	40	Bobby Hamilton	Kendall Pontiac
2	27	3	Dale Earnhardt	GM Goodwrench Chevrolet	23	32	29	Steve Grissom	Diamond Ridge Chevrolet
3	13	21	Morgan Shepherd	Citgo Ford	24	33	47	Billy Standridge	Standridge Auto Parts Ford
4	18	10	Ricky Rudd	Tide Ford	25	6	6	Mark Martin	Valvoline Ford
5	24	4	Sterling Marlin	Kodak Film Chevrolet	26	23	75	Todd Bodine	Factory Stores of America Ford
6	7	24	Jeff Gordon	DuPont Chevrolet	27	1	7	Geoff Bodine	Exide Batteries Ford
7	19	2	Rusty Wallace	Miller Genuine Draft Ford	28	38	71	Dave Marcis	Olive Garden Chevrolet
8	14	8	Jeff Burton	Raybestos Brakes Ford	29	5	26	Brett Bodine	Quaker State Ford
9	35	18	Dale Jarrett	Interstate Batteries Chevrolet	30	28	52	Brad Teague	Priddy's Lumber Ford
10	22	5	Terry Labonte	Kellogg's Corn Flakes Chevrolet	31	26	30	Michael Waltrip	Pennzoil Pontiac
11	11	28	Kenny Wallace	Texaco Havoline Ford	32	2	25	Ken Schrader	Kodak Chevrolet
12	37	42	Kyle Petty	Mello Yello Pontiac	33	25	98	Jeremy Mayfield	Fingerhut Ford
13	21	17	Darrell Waltrip	Western Auto Chevrolet	34	3	31	Ward Burton	Hardee's Chevrolet
14	36	23	Hut Stricklin	Smokin' Joe's Ford	35	20	12	Derrike Cope	Straight Arrow Ford
15	34	9	Phil Parsons	Melling Engine Parts Ford	36	8	22	Bobby Labonte	Maxwell House Coffee Pontiac
16	29	43	John Andretti	STP Pontiac	37	30	27	Jimmy Spencer	McDonald's Ford
17	39	90	Mike Wallace	Heilig-Meyers Ford	38	17	32	Dick Trickle	Active Trucking Chevrolet
18	41	55	Butch Miller	RaDiUs Ford	39	31	16	Ted Musgrave	The Family Channel Ford
19	12	77	Greg Sacks	USAir Ford	40	40	15	Lake Speed	Quality Care Ford
20	10	1	Rick Mast	Skoal Classic Ford	41	15	33	Harry Gant	Skoal Bandit Chevrolet
21	42	19	Loy Allen	Hooters Ford	42	4	41	Joe Nemechek	Meineke Mufflers Chevrolet

MILLER GENUINE DRAFT 400

RICHMOND
INTERNATIONAL RACEWAY

SEPTEMBER 10, 1994

Two days after his third career Mountain Dew Southern 500 victory, the most famous redhead to come out of north Georgia confirmed one of the worst-kept secrets in racing: Bill Elliott was returning to his hometown of Dawsonville and reuniting with his brothers, Dan and Ernie, for the 1995 season.

Bill said he would be part-owner of the new team with Georgia car dealer and businessman Charles Hardy, and their Fords would carry McDonald's sponsorship for '95 and beyond. The team, with several cars already built and more on the assembly line, would work from the Elliott shop just a couple of miles from the Dawsonville village square.

Elliott, bolstered by his recent victory and a string of solid finishes that had vaulted him from 18th to eighth in the Winston Cup standings, was jovial and easygoing at the Charlotte press conference. The Redhead had no chance to win the championship — he was more than 680 points behind — but he had proven in recent weeks that he still could get the job done behind the wheel. He was anxious to get started with his new team but would finish out the season with Junior Johnson and the Budweiser Ford.

With Elliott's long-rumored announcement now history, attention turned back to the annual Saturday "Showdown at Sundown" at the Sawyers' spectacular mini-superspeedway in Virginia's lovely capital city. Paul Sawyer and sons

(Top) Dick Trickle put together a solid run in the Active Trucking Chevrolet (32) to finish 12th in the Richmond sundowner. Dale Jarrett finished 16th. Michael Waltrip was seven laps behind in 26th place. (Right) The Richmond victory was Terry Labonte's second of the season; he also won earlier in the year at North Wilkesboro.

The field takes the green flag at Paul Sawyer's Richmond "mini-superspeedway." Ted Musgrave and Hut Stricklin were the surprising front-row tenants.

Wayne and Bill have continued to improve one of the tour's finest facilities — more than 79,000 seats now nearly encircle the three-quarter-mile oval.

The combination of Miller sponsoring the race, a brand-new mount waiting and crew chief Buddy Parrott signing up for two more years had Rusty Wallace on a high note at Richmond. He had used new cars each year — "Midnight" and "Midnight Rider" — to win the two previous runnings of this event and felt it was his time to make a move against point leader Dale Earnhardt. Wallace was 227 points behind with just eight races remaining; it was "crunch time" for the Penske driver.

Mark Martin's engine problem at Darlington put the Valvoline team in real point trouble. Mark now trailed by 283, and it was starting to look like another year would pass without the addition of a Winston Cup to the trophy case.

Except for smacking the wall at Michigan, Earnhardt's determined "return to racing" attitude had paid dividends. He had parried every thrust from Wallace and Martin in the last two races, finishing third at Bristol and second at Darlington. If he could continue to finish that

well, he wouldn't have to win a race for the remainder of the season. As far as he was concerned, no one was going to derail his freight-train run to a seventh championship.

With news of Ernie Irvan's continued improvement, drivers took to the track for qualifying with an eye on the track record. All except Elliott, that is. Elliott, suffering from a cyst over his right eye that had become infected, was in his hotel room receiving treatment. Veteran Busch Grand National star Tommy Houston was the driver selected by Junior Johnson to qualify Bill's Bud Ford in his absence.

Ted Musgrave, who drew the first number for qualifying,

While the race raged on, the McDonald's crew loaded Jimmy Spencer's car for the ride back to North Carolina. Spencer departed with ignition problems after 159 laps.

broke his own track record with his qualifying run. He then had to wait while everyone else attempted to knock him off the pole. They all failed, so the Family Channel Ford driver locked up his second career pole position. Alongside Musgrave was Hut Stricklin, whose Camel team was vindicated with the second-best time. (The team had failed to qualify for the spring Richmond race.)

The Brothers Labonte took the second row — Terry was barely faster than younger brother Bobby. Wallace debuted his yet unnamed chassis in the fifth-fastest lap. Greg Sacks, a hot-running Bobby Hamilton and rookie Steve Grissom took the next three spots, ahead of Geoff Bodine and Kenny Schrader. Earnhardt qualified 12th, and Mark Martin qualified right behind him with the 14th-fastest lap. Elliott, after attempting to qualify in the heat Saturday afternoon in the second round, took the provisional for the former champion, while Lake Speed and Jeremy Mayfield became the provisional starters for the 400-lapper. Those failing to make the field were: Billy Standridge, Dirk Stephens, Joe Ruttman, Phil Parsons (this week in the Melling Ford), Brad Teague and dirt-track racer Billy Ogle Jr.

Saturday, NASCAR's inspectors pulled the Stavola Brothers' Raybestos Ford from its stall and had the crew perform some surgery on part of the roll cage. The hoop running from the rear of the roll cage around the front of the car under the top of the windshield had been system-

Geoff Bodine hoped to challenge for the win, but he finished mid-field, three laps down to winner Terry Labonte.

John Andretti battled throughout the race and finished 11th, one lap behind, in the Petty Enterprises Pontiac. Here, he puts a lap on Dale Jarrett.

atically drilled, bringing the integrity of the roll cage into question. After a long discussion with the principal players of the team, the car and team were disqualified from the Richmond race. Raybestos moved its sponsorship to Steve Grissom's car for the night.

After a 90-minute rain delay, the race finally started. From the early going, it was evident that Terry Labonte's Kellogg's Chevrolet was the fastest car in the field. By the seventh lap, the Chevrolet was at the point, and

although Terry didn't lead all the laps, he led the majority of them. He had a brilliant night and dominated the race.

By the 350-lap mark, Terry had led nearly 200 laps. But he had one challenge left to overcome to seal his second victory of the season. Rusty's team had worked their magic on pit road on the final green-flag stop and turned the Miller driver back out after a 16.6-second stop. Terry's team tried to answer, but a broken air wrench cost an

Rick Mast and Derrike Cope go door-to-door under the Richmond lights.

extra five seconds, putting Terry at a huge disadvantage. But both the former champion and his Chevrolet were up to the challenge, and the Texan turned up the heat.

He made up those five seconds, caught Rusty with 26 laps to go and passed the black Ford. Wallace began to have engine problems with 12 laps remaining in the race and watched Jeff Gordon go by two laps later. Earnhardt, spotting Wallace in trouble ahead, floored his Chevrolet and passed Wallace on the next-to-last lap, dropping the Miller car to fourth. Ricky Rudd scrambled and clawed his way through the field, moving from 32nd to fifth, just ahead of Martin. Grissom finished seventh, the final car on the lead lap. Brett Bodine, Schrader and Darrell Waltrip claimed the final top-10 positions.

Terry's margin over Gordon was nearly 1.8 seconds. Earnhardt's third place, coupled with Wallace's fourth and Martin's sixth, gave him a tiny bit more breathing room at the top of the standings.

With Dover's Monster Mile on the horizon and only seven races left in the season, Earnhardt now commanded the top slot by 232 over Wallace and 303 over Martin.

It was Party Time for Terry Labonte and his team following the Richmond victory.

Fin. Pos.	Str. Pos.	Car #	Driver	Team	Fin. Pos.	Str. Pos.	Car #	Driver	Team
1	3	5	Terry Labonte	Kellogg's Corn Flakes Chevrolet	20	16	75	Todd Bodine	Factory Stores of America Ford
2	13	24	Jeff Gordon	DuPont Chevrolet	21	36	15	Lake Speed	Quality Care Ford
3	12	3	Dale Earnhardt	GM Goodwrench Chevrolet	22	31	33	Harry Gant	Skoal Bandit Chevrolet
4	5	2	Rusty Wallace	Miller Genuine Draft Ford	23	26	90	Mike Wallace	Heilig-Meyers Ford
5	32	10	Ricky Rudd	Tide Ford	24	4	22	Bobby Labonte	Maxwell House Coffee Pontiac
6	14	6	Mark Martin	Valvoline Ford	25	15	31	Ward Burton	Hardee's Chevrolet
7	8	29	Steve Grissom	Raybestos Brakes Chevrolet	26	20	30	Michael Waltrip	Pennzoil Pontiac
8	27	26	Brett Bodine	Quaker State Ford	27	6	77	Greg Sacks	USAir Ford
9	10	25	Ken Schrader	Kodiak Chevrolet	28	33	41	Joe Nemechek	Meineke Mufflers Chevrolet
10	29	17	Darrell Waltrip	Western Auto Chevrolet	29	22	71	Dave Marcis	Olive Garden Chevrolet
11	19	43	John Andretti	STP Pontiac	30	2	23	Hut Stricklin	Smokin' Joe's Ford
12	30	32	Dick Trickle	Active Trucking Chevrolet	31	35	19	Loy Allen	Hooters Ford
13	21	4	Sterling Marlin	Kodak Film Chevrolet	32	25	28	Kenny Wallace	Texaco Havoline Ford
14	28	21	Morgan Shepherd	Citgo Ford	33	11	1	Rick Mast	Skoal Classic Ford
15	38	11	Bill Elliott	Budweiser Ford	34	7	40	Bobby Hamilton	Kendall Pontiac
16	25	18	Dale Jarrett	Interstate Batteries Chevrolet	35	23	27	Jimmy Spencer	McDonald's Ford
17	1	16	Ted Musgrave	The Family Channel Ford	36	34	95	Jeff Green	Shoney's Ford
18	9	7	Geoff Bodine	Exide Batteries Ford	37	37	98	Jeremy Mayfield	Fingerhut Ford
19	18	12	Derrike Cope	Straight Arrow Ford	38	24	42	Kyle Petty	Mello Yello Pontiac

SPLITFIRE SPARK PLUG 500

DOVER DOWNS
INTERNATIONAL SPEEDWAY

SEPTEMBER 18, 1994

W hen the NASCAR Winston Cup tour assembled at Denis McGlynn's Dover Downs International Speedway for the Splitfire Spark Plug 500, competitors received news that gave them a two-fold sense of relief.

(Top) Rusty Wallace did everything he could to cut into Earnhardt's lead in the points, but he couldn't shake the six-time champion: They finished one-two. (Right) Rusty celebrates his seventh win of the season in Dover's victory lane.

Ernie Irvan had continued to improve, and he was allowed to transfer from an Ann Arbor, MI, hospital to a Charlotte rehabilitation facility near his home. Irvan had been admitted to the Michigan hospital after he suffered serious injuries in a practice-session wreck at Michigan International Speedway. The second item of good news was that the Splitfire Spark Plug 500 marked the last time drivers would race on the current Dover surface.

Since NASCAR sanctioned racing at Dover in 1969, the track rightfully had earned its "Monster Mile" nickname, proving through the years to be one of the most grueling and difficult tracks on the circuit. The completion of 500 laps at Dover, with its roller coaster entries and exits to its corners, was a task that demanded the utmost concentration from every driver. A slip by anyone usually meant that several drivers, not just the driver at fault, would be collected for a meeting with the concrete wall.

The management at Dover announced that the track would be redesigned slightly and resurfaced with concrete by the time the teams returned for the early June race in 1995.

DuPont, located just 45 minutes north of the Dover track, announced it would extend its sponsorship of the "24" car

Mark Martin's Valvoline Ford blew a tire and smacked the wall six laps from the end of the race. The late-race turn of events was a bitter pill for Mark; he had been firmly in the lead and on the way to his first-ever win at the Monster Mile.

until the year 2000. During that announcement, Rick Hendrick made sure that everyone concerned knew that his contract with driver Jeff Gordon ran through 1998 – just in case anyone wanted to try to "raid" his Hendrick Motorsport camp!

Kenny Bernstein, searching for a driver to replace Brett Bodine in 1995, reached outside the "normal" NASCAR Winston Cup pool and signed 13-time World of Outlaws Sprint Car king Steve Kinser. Ward Burton, rumored to be a candidate for several vacant top rides for next season, took himself out of the mix by stating that he would remain with the A.G. Dillard team and that Hardee's would continue its sponsorship in 1995. Rumors that Kenny Schrader would carry the red and white Budweiser colors next season if Hendrick could find a suitable place for the Kodiak sponsorship (which had a year remaining on Schrader's car) were circulating throughout the garage. And Brett Bodine appeared to be in the driver's seat for the Junior Johnson ride in '95. First, though, Junior had to find a sponsor to replace departing McDonald's, which was headed for Dawsonville with Bill Elliott. Jimmy Spencer, the winner of two races so far in 1994, appeared headed for the

Travis Carter/Smokin' Joe's team. RaDiUs Racing, after releasing Jimmy Hensley after the Bristol race, was trying its third driver in three events: Tim Fedewa would try to make the Dover field in the "55" Ford.

The biggest news, however, was that Jeff Burton would assume a larger role with the Stavola Brothers' Ford. This development occurred after crew chief and engine-builder Ken Wilson resigned.

Throughout the season, the combination of Hoosier tires, Geoff Bodine's chassis work, crew preparation and stout engines have made the Exide Ford one of the fastest cars on the track. And by qualifying's end, Bodine had won his fifth pole of the season. The black and blue Ford at the top of the list was no surprise, but the identity of the driver who shared the front row was a shocker.

Dick Trickle had slapped his Chevrolet in the second starting spot, missing the pole by a few hundredths of a second. Behind him were Ward Burton and Mark Martin, and in the third row were Brett Bodine and Jeff Burton. Kenny Wallace and Rick Mast turned in the seventh- and eighth-fastest times, and Todd Bodine and Rusty Wallace claimed the final top 10 positions.

Point leader Dale Earnhardt was struggling in his

"bullet-proofed" Chevrolet. After two rounds of qualifying, he was way back for the start in 37th place. Fedewa made the field in his debut with the RaDiUs Ford. Occasional NASCAR Winston Cup competitors Norm Benning, Doug French and Billy Standridge, however, did not have any provisional starting positions available to them, and all three were forced to go home and watch the race on The Nashville Network.

The presence of the Brothers Bodine, Burton and Wallace (Kenny and Rusty) in the top 10 to start the race set a record even before the flag dropped: It was the first time in NASCAR history that three sets of brothers had qualified within the first 10 positions for a NASCAR Winston Cup race.

After the green flag dropped, Geoff Bodine left no doubt that his qualifying lap was a true indication of his Ford's strength. He ripped away to lead all but 10 of the first 180 laps. However, just 40 laps later, at mid-distance, Earnhardt emerged as the race leader after masterfully working his way through the field. When Geoff lost the handle on his Ford, the race turned into a second-half battle between Rusty, Dale and Martin, who was looking for his second win of the season. Darrell Waltrip led while the other pace-setters pitted under green for tires and fuel, but in the final 100 laps, Mark pulled away from the field and built a seven-second lead with just over 20 laps to go. It looked like he had finally solved the Dover puzzle.

But Martin had a brush with Ricky Rudd when he passed the two-laps-down Tide Ford, and he slowed slightly on the track to make sure his Valvoline Ford was all right. As he did so, Wallace began shortening the

(Left) You've heard of the lion tamer sticking his head in the lion's mouth? Michael Waltrip puts a new spin on the old circus trick. (Below) The Bahari team worked hard throughout the season to stay within striking distance of the top ten in Winston Cup points. The determination of Waltrip and his crew was depicted when they returned a modified Pennzoil Pontiac to the track after an early-race altercation.

Dover's high banks allow two-abreast racing in the turns. Jeff Gordon and Derrike Cope (12) duke it out late in the race; in the end, Gordon and Cope would finish in eleventh and twelfth place, respectively.

distance between the two Fords. As a determined Rusty closed in on him, Mark's right-front tire – cut by the sheetmetal pushed in during the brush with Rudd – let go. With just five laps left, Mark scraped into the wall, Rusty slashed past and the yellow flew. Right behind Wallace was Earnhardt, and everyone expected the track to be cleared for a final dash to determine the winner.

Then it all fell apart. Rick Mast's Skoal Ford stalled on the apron of the first turn, and as soon as a wrecker headed for it, Sterling Marlin's Kodak Chevrolet stalled on the exit to pit road. The race would finish under yellow, but no one could guess who would win! Wallace clung to the apron all around the track, trying to keep his out-of-gas Ford

Wallace's tire shows signs of wear after the finish of the Splitfire 500. Rusty's tire went flat after he ran over debris from Martin's wreck on lap 494. Luckily for Rusty, the race finished under caution, and he was able to nurse the Miller Ford home behind the pace car.

running. He also had a flat tire – he had run over a piece of brake caliper. And behind him, Earnhardt hugged the apron as well, trying to keep his Chevrolet running on fumes. Darrell Waltrip was cruising in third. If the two black cars in front of him faltered, the three-time champion could make his first trip to victory lane since Darlington's 1992 Mountain Dew Southern 500.

But Darrell would have to wait. Rusty and Dale made it to the checkered flag, although both were creeping along the track behind Elmo Langley and the Pontiac pace car.

The bizarre final laps also ended Trickle's splendid bid. Trickle, who had been running seventh after spending the day in the top 10, cut a tire with nine laps remaining, and struggled home 21st, six laps behind.

Behind Waltrip, Schrader posted his eighth top five of the season. Geoff was right behind Schrader. Kyle Petty produced one of his better runs of the year to come home sixth, ahead of Richmond winner Terry Labonte and Steve Grissom, the highest-finishing MAXX rookie contender. Lake Speed and Morgan Shepherd completed the top 10.

Geoff Bodine gives his crew – many of whom remain from the days when Alan Kulwicki owned the team – much of the credit for his success during his rookie year as an owner/driver. With their help, Bodine started from the pole and led throughout most of the race's first half.

Fin. Pos.	Str. Pos.	Car #	Driver	Team	Fin. Pos.	Str. Pos.	Car #	Driver	Team
1	10	2	Rusty Wallace	Miller Genuine Draft Ford	21	2	32	Dick Trickle	Active Trucking Chevrolet
2	37	3	Dale Earnhardt	GM Goodwrench Chevrolet	22	40	19	Loy Allen	Hooters Ford
3	35	17	Darrell Waltrip	Western Auto Chevrolet	23	38	55	Tim Fedewa	RaDiUs Racing Ford
4	14	25	Ken Schrader	Kodiak Chevrolet	24	33	98	Jeremy Mayfield	Fingerhut Ford
5	1	7	Geoff Bodine	Exide Batteries Ford	25	23	43	John Andretti	STP Pontiac
6	15	42	Kyle Petty	Mello Yello Pontiac	26	5	26	Brett Bodine	Quaker State Ford
7	29	5	Terry Labonte	Kellogg's Corn Flakes Chevrolet	27	3	31	Ward Burton	Hardee's Chevrolet
8	34	29	Steve Grissom	Diamond Ridge Chevrolet	28	13	11	Bill Elliott	Budweiser Ford
9	22	15	Lake Speed	Quality Care Ford	29	25	90	Mike Wallace	Heilig-Meyers Ford
10	20	21	Morgan Shepherd	Citgo Ford	30	18	4	Sterling Marlin	Kodak Film Chevrolet
11	12	24	Jeff Gordon	DuPont Chevrolet	31	11	40	Bobby Hamilton	Kendall Pontiac
12	17	12	Derrike Cope	Straight Arrow Ford	32	32	23	Hut Stricklin	Smokin' Joe's Ford
13	30	33	Harry Gant	Skoal Bandit Chevrolet	33	28	30	Michael Waltrip	Pennzoil Pontiac
14	26	16	Ted Musgrave	The Family Channel Ford	34	19	18	Dale Jarrett	Interstate Batteries Chevrolet
15	8	1	Rick Mast	Skoal Classic Ford	35	24	71	Dave Marcis	Olive Garden Chevrolet
16	9	75	Todd Bodine	Factory Stores of America Ford	36	21	41	Joe Nemechek	Meineke Mufflers Chevrolet
17	31	22	Bobby Labonte	Maxwell House Coffee Pontiac	37	6	8	Jeff Burton	Raybestos Brakes Ford
18	16	10	Ricky Rudd	Tide Ford	38	36	77	Greg Sacks	USAir Ford
19	4	6	Mark Martin	Valvoline Ford	39	27	27	Jimmy Spencer	McDonald's Ford
20	7	28	Kenny Wallace	Texaco Havoline Ford	40	39	52	Brad Teague	Bender Plastics Ford

GOODY'S 500

MARTINSVILLE SPEEDWAY  SEPTEMBER 25, 1994

After his victory at Dover, Rusty Wallace found himself heading to Martinsville with mixed emotions. He was in the middle of a torrid streak: In five races, he had notched his sixth and seventh victories, finished fourth twice and seventh once. When Dale Earnhardt finished the Michigan race in 37th place due to a wreck, Wallace managed to come within 213 points of Earnhardt. Wallace thought he had a real, fighting chance to close the gap on the black Chevrolet and put himself in a position to challenge for the NASCAR Winston Cup title in the year's final races.

As the tour had wound its way through Bristol, Darlington, Richmond and Dover, the Miller Ford driver had done his job, and his Penske South crew had done theirs.

But Wallace merely had to look at the point standings posted on the NASCAR trailer in the garage area at Martinsville to see the real effect of his five-race string.

The Goodwrench team also had turned up its efforts a notch after the Michigan mess, and Earnhardt was taking no prisoners with his two second-place finishes and two third-place finishes in the last four races. The black Chevrolet hadn't found its way into victory lane – which rankled the six-time champion – but the effort had not only kept

(Top) It was fitting that Rusty, who had amassed a series-leading eight victories, was the one to clinch the Manufacturer's Championship for Ford. Rusty celebrates in victory lane after the Goody's 500 with Ford's Preston Miller (left) and Penske Racing South co-owner Don Miller. (Right) Bill Elliott enjoys a moment of solitude before beginning his 500-lap run on the Martinsville, VA, half-miler. The Budweiser Ford driver ran well and finished third.

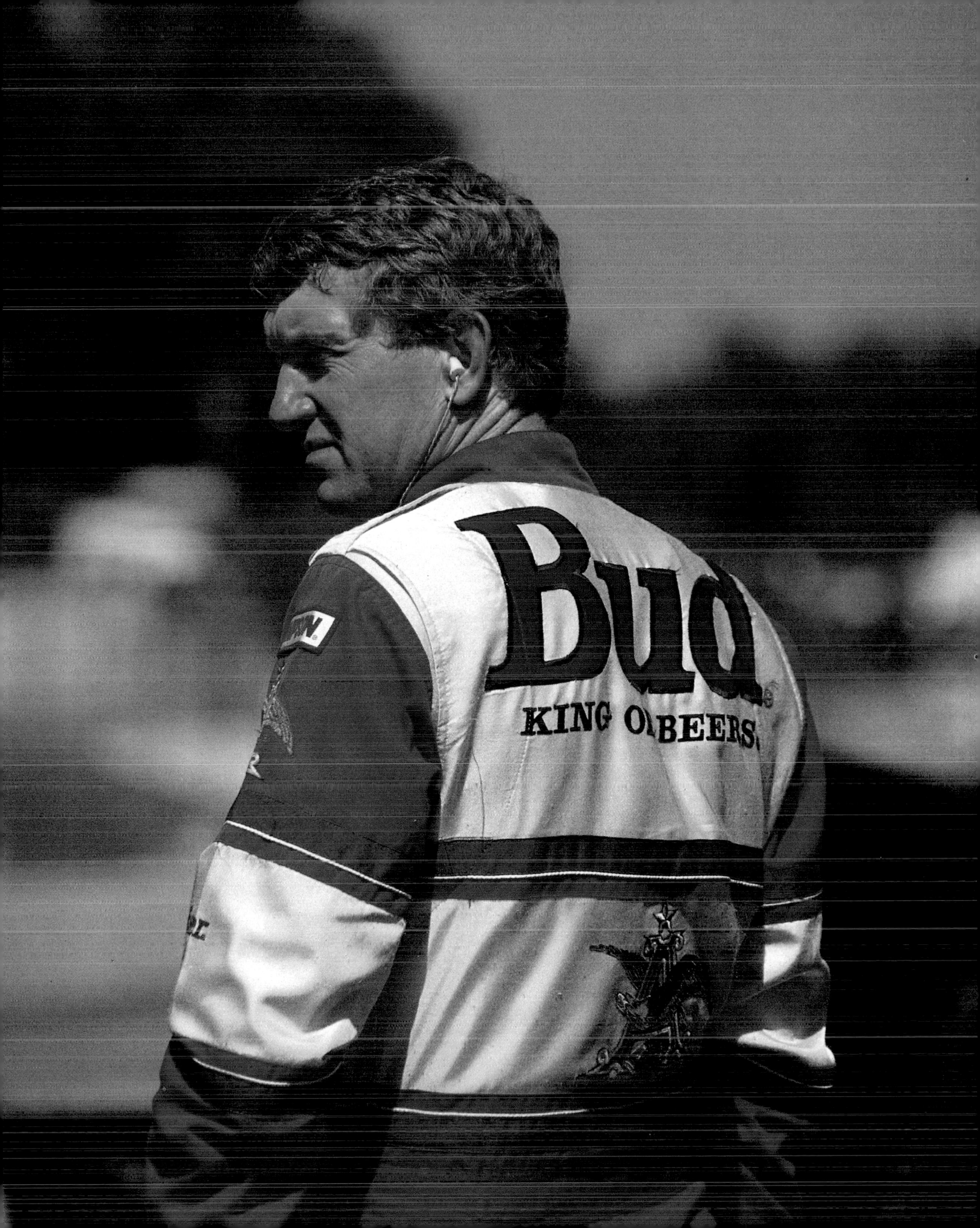
Bud

Wallace from cutting further into the lead but padded Dale's advantage by an additional 14 points during the four races.

The four races since Michigan had left a sour taste in Mark Martin's mouth. He had had the Mountain Dew Southern 500 in hand until his engine blew with 25 laps to go, and at Dover, a cut tire cost him another victory. More importantly, he had

fallen from 206 to 367 points behind Earnhardt; Mark knew that any chance of realizing his dream of winning his first title had been postponed until next year.

As the teams prepared for qualifying, media members asked Rusty if he still felt he had a chance to win the title. Rusty not only had seven victories to point to, but he also was proud to say that the Penske team had been instrumental in putting Ford Motor Company into a position to be able to clinch NASCAR's Manufacturer's Championship within the next two races. A single victory by a Ford team would bring the Blue Oval folks their second title in the last three years.

After qualifying at Martinsville had been completed, Ted Musgrave gave serious thought to moving his residence a few miles north, from North Carolina to Virginia. The Family Channel Ford driver had won his third 1994 pole in four tries on Virginia soil and given his Robin Pemberton-led team something to celebrate with

With six races remaining in "The Bandit's Last Ride" farewell tour, Harry Gant wanted nothing more than to visit victory lane once more.

two poles in the last three races!

Geoff Bodine again was quick with his Exide Ford and claimed the outside of the first row. Jeff Burton had shaken off his Dover accident to qualify third, and John Andretti continued to impress, making the fourth-fastest lap in Richard Petty's STP Pontiac. Martin and Jeff Gordon made up the third row, followed by Rusty and Dale Jarrett, who posted his best qualifying effort of the year. Sterling Marlin and Bill Elliott completed the fifth row. Once again, teams had to look a long way down the list to find the point leader. Earnhardt was only 20th-fastest, and Rick Mast and Mike Wallace were forced to use provisionals to get into the field. Dave Marcis, Bobby Hillin, Loy Allen, Tim Fedewa and Jeremy Mayfield went home.

When race day dawned, Rusty slid behind the wheel of his street car and headed for Clay Earles and Clay Campbell's splendid little half-mile. There was only one thing to think about during the trip to the track. He knew he had to continue running at the front, win races and score as many points as he could. That was all he could do: score the most points each week and hope that at some point, Earnhardt's torrid tear would come to an end.

After the green flag dropped, Wallace patiently started working his way toward the front. On the 34th lap, he thought his hopes had been answered. Earnhardt and Kenny Wallace collided, and Dale looped the black Chevrolet in a smoke-filled, power-induced 360. Instead of being tangled with others, however, as usually happens at Martinsville, Dale merely motored away, losing only some rubber off his Goodyears. Some 40 laps later, Rick Mast cut a tire and collected Earnhardt, but Dale again was able to carry on.

When Rusty moved to the point on lap 112 and began to dominate the remainder of the race, Earnhardt gave chase. Wallace cut a tire with just over 50 laps to go and dove for pit road. When others came in for green-flag stops a lap later, he was right back in the hunt for the win.

Ted Musgrave led the field from the pole – his third of the year. Although he appears to be the sole occupant of the front row, he was not alone: Geoff Bodine, hidden from view, was his front-row companion.

Morgan Shepherd's spin on lap 459 brought out the final yellow of the day, and the stage was set for the battle to the finish when leader Jeff Gordon allowed Wallace out of the pits first after an air-wrench malfunction. Elliott's team beat Earnhardt's in the pit road battle, but when the green flew for the last time, Dale ducked past Elliott and went after Wallace with all he had.

They bumped. They banged. Dale slashed. Rusty parried. Thump! Crunch! Bip! Bam!

It was the stuff that has made NASCAR Winston Cup the greatest form of racing in the world. Two equally matched cars. Ford versus Chevrolet. A pair of lion-hearted drivers in the prime of their careers. No quarter asked, none given. No time-outs. No plays from the bench. Just get it on!

No wonder ESPN had been delighted to announce a long extension of its contract with Martinsville before the race!

Lap after lap, Dale tried to find a way to dislodge Rusty from the point. Wallace refused to give up the lead. Finally, Earnhardt, his brakes cooked with only three laps left, faded slightly, and Rusty came home four car-lengths ahead for his eighth win of the year.

Darrell Waltrip found the perfect spot for uninterrupted pre-race preparation at Martinsville. Waltrip and his crew had reassessed their approach in the final third of the season, and their new focus and intensity had been rewarded with a series of good finishes. Their 10th-place finish in the Goody's 500 proved that persistence pays.

But all his efforts resulted in only a measly 10-point gain in the standings. With five races left, Rusty was still 217 behind.

But there were still plenty of reasons to celebrate. Wallace collected another grandfather clock, symbolic of his victory, and he pulled his driver's suit off his shoulders and yanked on a tee shirt. It bore a blue Ford oval and the words "1994 NASCAR Manufacturer's Champion." The splendid win had iced the title for the Dearborn folks and had provided them with an honored place on the stage at the Waldorf-Astoria in December – even if a Chevrolet driver ended up with the Winston Cup crown.

Behind the pace-setting Wallace-Earnhardt sheetmetal fisticuffs came Elliott, continuing the hot string that had moved him from 18th to eighth in the standings. Kenny Wallace recorded his best career finish: a fourth in the Havoline Ford. Jarrett, driving one-handed due to a fractured bone in his wrist, managed a fifth-place finish. Kenny Schrader fought his way to sixth, ahead of Marlin, and Harry Gant posted an eighth place in his final Martinsville outing. Musgrave came home ninth, and Darrell Waltrip posted his seventh top 10 in the last eight races. Waltrip had climbed from 16th to ninth in the point standings.

Short-track racing at Martinsville is door-to-door, fender-to-fender competition. Ken Schrader (25) and Ted Musgrave show the fans how it's done.

Fin. Pos.	Str. Pos.	Car #	Driver	Team		Fin. Pos.	Str. Pos.	Car #	Driver	Team
1	7	2	Rusty Wallace	Miller Genuine Draft Ford		19	31	30	Michael Waltrip	Pennzoil Pontiac
2	20	3	Dale Earnhardt	GM Goodwrench Chevrolet		20	28	27	Jimmy Spencer	McDonald's Ford
3	10	11	Bill Elliott	Budweiser Ford		21	4	43	John Andretti	STP Pontiac
4	12	28	Kenny Wallace	Texaco Havoline Ford		22	26	41	Joe Nemechek	Meineke Mufflers Chevrolet
5	8	18	Dale Jarrett	Interstate Batteries Chevrolet		23	21	23	Hut Stricklin	Smokin' Joe's Ford
6	14	25	Ken Schrader	Kodiak Chevrolet		24	16	42	Kyle Petty	Mello Yello Pontiac
7	9	4	Sterling Marlin	Kodak Film Chevrolet		25	13	10	Ricky Rudd	Tide Ford
8	24	33	Harry Gant	Skoal Bandit Chevrolet		26	34	77	Greg Sacks	USAir Ford
9	1	16	Ted Musgrave	The Family Channel Ford		27	32	52	Brad Teague	Means Racing Ford
10	11	17	Darrell Waltrip	Western Auto Chevrolet		28	36	90	Mike Wallace	Heilig-Meyers Ford
11	6	24	Jeff Gordon	DuPont Chevrolet		29	35	1	Rick Mast	Skoal Classic Ford
12	30	29	Steve Grissom	Diamond Ridge Chevrolet		30	25	26	Brett Bodine	Quaker State Ford
13	29	40	Bobby Hamilton	Kendall Pontiac		31	22	22	Bobby Labonte	Maxwell House Coffee Pontiac
14	17	5	Terry Labonte	Kellogg's Corn Flakes Chevrolet		32	27	32	Dick Trickle	Active Trucking Chevrolet
15	23	21	Morgan Shepherd	Citgo Ford		33	33	75	Todd Bodine	Factory Stores of America Ford
16	5	6	Mark Martin	Valvoline Ford		34	15	15	Lake Speed	Quality Care Ford
17	19	12	Derrike Cope	Straight Arrow Ford		35	18	31	Ward Burton	Hardee's Chevrolet
18	2	7	Geoff Bodine	Exide Batteries Ford		36	3	8	Jeff Burton	Raybestos Brakes Ford

TYSON HOLLY FARMS 400

NORTH WILKESBORO SPEEDWAY   OCTOBER 2, 1994

With the ninth of ten consecutive races staring them in the face, teams unloaded at North Wilkesboro for the Tyson Holly Farms 400, hosted on the five-eighths-mile oval located in the foothills of North Carolina's Brushy Mountains.

For some, the stretch run for this year's NASCAR Winston Cup had been a rewarding effort. For others, the nightmare seemed to continue race after race. Dale Earnhardt had protected his lead, which he had regained at Indy in early August. With Ernie Irvan unable to compete, Dale had climbed to 217 points ahead of second-place Rusty Wallace. Meanwhile, Mark Martin continued to fall away, now trailing by 427. Mark, instead of battling for the NASCAR Winston Cup as he had hoped, now was looking over his shoulder. A pair of drivers – Kenny Schrader and Ricky Rudd – were closing in on him fast, intent on overtaking the third-place position he now occupied in the point standings.

Morgan Shepherd was sixth – exactly the same place he was in when the string began – and Jeff Gordon had continued his strong showings by moving from ninth at the beginning of the string to seventh headed into North Wilkesboro. Bill Elliott, Darrell Waltrip and Terry Labonte had used the series of races to their advantage, climbing into eighth, ninth and 10th places from 12th, 16th and 14th, respectively.

(Top) One of the advantages of driving your own car: more trophies! Geoff is either very happy or straining to hang on to all that hardware! Bodine smoked the field, leading the last 300 laps, and finished on the lead lap by himself. (Right) In the latter stages of the race, Ricky Rudd, Kenny Wallace and Ted Musgrave fight hard for position. Musgrave was able to work his Family Channel Thunderbird past the other Fords to finish ninth, and Kenny managed to pass Rudd for tenth. The Tide Ford was relegated to 11th place.

Mark Martin and Rusty Wallace clearly are capable of expressing their intensity without words.

Michael Waltrip had posted only one top 10 finish (seventh at Bristol) in the seven races since the Brickyard, and the fortunes of the Pennzoil Pontiac had plummeted. Michael had fallen from eighth to 12th in the standings and lost 377 points during the seven race string.

Teams were heartened by Ernie's release from a Charlotte hospital although the driver would continue intensive therapy sessions. No one was certain when Ernie would be able to return to racing, so Robert Yates was forced to begin thinking about a suitable replacement for Ernie in 1995. The "28" car became a hotspot in the "silly season" rumor mill. Bobby Labonte's status in 1995 also became grist for the rumor mill.

A press conference was scheduled for the Tuesday following the North Wilkesboro race to announce Budweiser's move to the Hendrick team and sponsorship of Kenny Schrader. Kenny had other issues on his mind, however. His father, William, a Midwest short-track terror in his own right, had died at the age of 75 on the Wednesday before the race. For five days, Kenny's plane flew back and forth between North Wilkesboro and St. Louis.

Rick Hendrick had apparently worked things out with Kodiak; the company was expected to move its green

A split second saved on pit road can translate into crucial gains on the track. The "Flying Aces" use video equipment to help them perfect their choreography in the pits.

Jimmy Spencer and Bill Elliott swept the front row for the start of the Holly Farms 400 in their Junior Johnson Fords. The fact that North Wilkesboro is Junior's home track was just icing on the cake. (Johnson's team shops are located just a few miles away in Ingles Hollow, NC.)

completed Friday, Junior and his teams had plenty of reason to strut as they left the infield. Jimmy Spencer had slapped the McDonald's Ford on the pole for the first time in his career, and Bill Elliott barely had missed unseating Spencer. The Budweiser Ford had captured the outside of the front row, just .001 of a second slower than the McDonald's Ford.

After failing to qualify in the top 10 in six consecutive races, Earnhardt found himself third alongside Martin's Valvoline Ford. There were plenty of surprises behind them. Jeff Green, normally Michael Waltrip's race day spotter, hustled the Sadler Racing Ford to the fifth starting position, and Dave Marcis was planted outside Green in the third row. Darrell proved his team was coming together, notching his best qualifying effort of the year with the seventh starting position on the grid. He was inside Bobby Hamilton, who had the fastest Pontiac. Morgan Shepherd and

and white colors to Larry Hedrick's team for 1995. Joe Nemechek said he would field his own Winston Cup team for the '95 season (with Richard Childress' engines) and left the "41" open for the right deal. NASCAR Busch Grand National series hotshoe Ricky Craven became the logical choice for the Hedrick team's Chevrolets.

Junior Johnson, whose race shop is just a few miles down the road and whose history began with a victory at North Wilkesboro in 1958, has always been determined to have his cars run well in his "backyard." His 18 victories at the track over the years are a testament to his team's ability to adjust to the vagaries of the uphill\downhill North Wilkesboro oval.

After the first round of qualifying had been

Crew chief Donnie Richeson consults with Brett Bodine before the start of the Holly Farms 400. The car suffered mechanical problems during the race, resulting in a 33rd-place finish.

Lake Speed took provisionals to get into the field. Mike Wallace, Loy Allen, Tim Fedewa and Brad Teague, unable to net the necessary speed, went home to watch the race on television. Accompanying them were Dale Jarrett and Todd Bodine, both of whom had failed to make a field for the first time all year.

No one could have envisioned what would unfold during the 400 laps. Geoff Bodine simply took everyone behind the woodshed, becoming the first driver to lap the field since Harry Gant's dominant victory at Dover in September 1991.

It took Geoff 58 laps to move to the point but from then on, with the exception of 18 laps when he fell out of the lead due to green-flag stops, he led the remainder of the event. It was an awesome display of chassis, power, tires, pit work and driving skill, and no one had anything for the owner\driver of the Exide Ford. During the first 329 laps, all under green, Geoff simply motored away from the field. By the time the first caution came out everyone was a lap down, and Geoff had pit road all to himself for his first yellow-flag stop. Terry Labonte did the best he could to contest Bodine, moving past the Ford to gain the tail of the lead lap on lap 367, but no caution emerged and Geoff passed him back 15 laps later.

The remainder of the field fought for the scraps behind them. Rick Mast matched his best finish of the year (August at Michigan) with a third place, and Rusty came home fourth ahead of Martin, Elliott and Earnhardt. Wallace gained nine points in the point chase. He had hoped to gain more when Dale damaged the right front of his Goodwrench Chevrolet in a scramble with Jeff Burton on a restart, but Earnhardt's team provided quick and effective service. Dale continued his march toward his record-tying seventh championship. He finished two laps down but put himself in the position of needing to finish only 10th or better in the remaining races to claim the crown.

Jeff Gordon was eighth, followed by Ted Musgrave and Kenny Wallace, who completed the top 10. Hensley, in relief of Kyle after 112 laps, was involved in a wreck when Sterling Marlin's Kodak Chevrolet blew up while running underneath the Mello Yello Pontiac and carried both cars into the wall.

Normally, teams would be relieved that the final race in the stretch run, the Mello Yello 500 at Charlotte, awaited them. However, Charlotte had been repaved since the May race, and no one knew exactly what to expect from the 1.5-mile superspeedway.

Some accused Dale Earnhardt of driving conservatively to protect his lead in the points. Dale never acquiesced and demonstrated that he hadn't slowed one bit by "threading the needle" between Jeff Green (95) and Bobby Labonte on North Wilkesboro's five-eighths-mile short track.

The Kellogg's crew, led by Gary DeHart, helped Terry Labonte drive to a second-place finish. No one could challenge Geoff Bodine, but Terry was the "best of the rest."

Fin. Pos.	Str. Pos.	Car #	Driver	Team	Fin. Pos.	Str. Pos.	Car #	Driver	Team
1	18	7	Geoff Bodine	Exide Batteries Ford	19	16	12	Derrike Cope	Straight Arrow Ford
2	10	5	Terry Labonte	Kellogg's Chevrolet	20	33	29	Steve Grissom	Channellock Chevrolet
3	17	1	Rick Mast	Skoal Classic Ford	21	13	30	Michael Waltrip	Pennzoil Pontiac
4	19	2	Rusty Wallace	Miller Genuine Draft Ford	22	25	23	Hut Stricklin	Smokin' Joe's Ford
5	4	6	Mark Martin	Valvoline Ford	23	1	27	Jimmy Spencer	McDonald's Ford
6	2	11	Bill Elliott	Budweiser Ford	24	6	71	Dave Marcis	Olive Garden Chevrolet
7	3	3	Dale Earnhardt	GM Goodwrench Chevrolet	25	36	15	Lake Speed	Ford Quality Care Ford
8	12	24	Jeff Gordon	DuPont Chevrolet	26	22	42	Kyle Petty	Mello Yello Pontiac
9	29	16	Ted Musgrave	The Family Channel Ford	27	34	98	Jeremy Mayfield	Fingerhut Ford
10	9	28	Kenny Wallace	Texaco Havoline Ford	28	14	8	Jeff Burton	Raybestos Brakes Ford
11	26	10	Ricky Rudd	Tide Ford	29	5	95	Jeff Green	Shoney's Ford
12	8	40	Bobby Hamilton	Kendall Pontiac	30	35	21	Morgan Shepherd	Citgo Ford
13	7	17	Darrell Waltrip	Western Auto Chevrolet	31	24	4	Sterling Marlin	Kodak Film Chevrolet
14	27	25	Ken Schrader	Kodiak Chevrolet	32	23	33	Harry Gant	Skoal Bandit Chevrolet
15	20	22	Bobby Labonte	Maxwell House Pontiac	33	15	26	Brett Bodine	Quaker State Ford
16	31	32	Dick Trickle	Active Trucking Chevrolet	34	32	41	Joe Nemechek	Meineke Mufflers Chevrolet
17	28	43	John Andretti	STP Pontiac	35	11	77	Greg Sacks	USAir Ford
18	21	31	Ward Burton	Hardee's Chevrolet	36	30	9	Phil Parsons	Melling Racing Ford

MELLO YELLO 500

After Geoff Bodine gave the field a whipping at North Wilkesboro, teams were anxious to unload at Charlotte for the last-ever Mello Yello 500; they hoped to even the score with the Exide Ford and its driver. CMS had repaved its 1.5-mile track, and the new surface rendered the old chassis "black books" useless, so most crew chiefs thought everyone would be on reasonably equal terms for qualifying and the 500-miler.

Traditionally, the fall event at Charlotte is used to lay the groundwork for the coming season. Sponsors take advantage of the large media turnout to make announcements regarding the next year, and usually, driver changes take the spotlight. This year's event supported that trend, but at the same time, more questions popped up than were answered concerning driver/sponsor partnerships.

Junior Johnson and the Lowe's people made their long-anticipated announcement regarding Brett Bodine driving the "11" car for the coming season, and Jimmy Spencer was named the driver for the '95 Smokin' Joe's effort. Derrike Cope signed on for the full Cup season and a limited Busch season with the Bobby Allison/Ron Zook race team. But that's where the answers stopped.

Car owner Felix Sabates announced that he was severing his ties with the Coca-Cola Company and its Mello Yello brand. Just a year earlier, Sabates and Coca-Cola had announced they would be together through the year 2000. Felix said he had another sponsor ready to sign and that Kyle Petty would remain with the Pontiac team for '95.

(Top) Ward Burton and Michael Waltrip bring the field to the starting line to take the green flag in the Mello Yello 500. (Right) Dale Jarrett is elated after his win in the Mello Yello 500; he fought hard throughout the race to earn his first victory since the 1993 Daytona 500.

MELLO YELLO
500
CHARLOTTE MOTOR SPEEDWAY
NASCAR
Winston Cu
INTERSTATE BATTERIES
18
LUMINA

Ernie Irvan attended the race – the first since his accident. Meanwhile, Robert Yates and company tried to figure out what to do for '95. Yates Racing would field a Ford for Ernie when the time came, but in the meantime, Yates "was taking resumes" for the full-time seat in the Havoline Ford. Dale Jarrett's name became associated with the rumors.

Fifty-four entries were attempting to qualify for the last race Mello Yello would sponsor in Charlotte, and it was obvious that many teams would be disappointed. Many drivers would wind up watching the race on television when the NASCAR Winston Cup field took the green flag Sunday. Qualifying continued to be of paramount importance: For many teams, making the field became more important than how well they ran in the race on Sunday!

During the first session, run Wednesday evening under the lights, the top 10 was filled with surprises. Ward Burton continued his habit of qualifying well at Charlotte. With Hoosiers on his Hardee's Chevrolet, Ward claimed the pole at nearly 186 miles per hour. That was more than four mph faster than Joe Nemechek's record which was set in May for the Winston Select Open! The record-trashing continued; in all, 16 drivers surpassed Nemechek's mark!

The crowd had anticipated a classic duel between these two longtime rivals, and a battle had appeared to be taking shape. Unfortunately, the fans were disappointed: Rusty's engine expired, and he was forced to watch the remainder of the race from the garage area. Dale forged on and finished third.

Michael Waltrip nearly won the pole, but he could only watch as Ward, next-to-last in line, beat the Pennzoil Pontiac by two-tenths of a second. John Andretti was another surprise, claiming the inside of the second row alongside Nemechek. Jeff Gordon, the winner of the May race, was fifth-fastest, and Geoff Bodine was on his right. Cope, with his first new car since signing on with Bobby Allison's team at Watkins Glen, responded with a seventh-fastest time, inside Brett Bodine. Terry Labonte and a fast-running Dick Trickle

finished off the top 10. Rusty Wallace, desperately trying to get back into the point battle, qualified 15th. Point leader Dale Earnhardt would start 38th in his Goodwrench Chevrolet.

Steve Grissom – carrying Sears' DieHard batteries colors for the first time – and Kyle Petty used the provisionals, and 12 teams were forced to load up their transporters after qualifying. Those failing to make the field were: Dave Marcis, Phil Parsons, Ken Bouchard, Butch Miller, Brad Noffsinger, Brad Teague, Pancho Carter, Kirk Shelmerdine, Norm Benning, Ben Hess and Rich Bickle.

No one had to tell Rusty what he had to do in Sunday's race. He was more than 200 points behind, and there were only four races left in the season. He needed to run at the front and hope Earnhardt had some problems more than once. Otherwise, the Miller driver was destined for another runner-up season despite his eight victories.

Five laps into the race, it looked like Rusty's luck had turned. Bobby

Competitors and fans alike were delighted to see Ernie Irvan at CMS. Irvan had suffered severe injuries at Michigan just seven weeks prior to the Mello Yello 500.

Labonte had an accident, and Earnhardt tangled with Bill Elliott while trying to avoid the wreckage. Earnhardt headed for pit road with right-front damage, but the Flying Aces answered the call. Dale returned to the track on the lead lap and fought his way through the field. He ultimately took the point for a total of six laps, and Wallace's title dreams took another clubbing when the black and yellow Ford exited after 256 laps with a broken timing chain. Wallace now trailed by 321, and Dale was in position to claim his seventh crown at Rockingham.

Once Geoff Bodine established himself at the front of the field, it looked like another dominant win was in the cards for the car owner and driver. Behind him, the battle raged for the second spot, and a handful of cars looked capable of winning if Bodine had problems. He did – the engine died with 48 laps to go after he had led 202 of the 286 laps – and the race turned into a serious dogfight.

With 34 laps to go, leader Brett Bodine pitted for four tires. Kenny Schrader, hoping for his first win of the year, was at the point. Behind him, Jarrett, Morgan Shepherd and Earnhardt were locked in a furious struggle. Earnhardt pitted for right sides with 25 laps to go, and Jarrett hit pit lane two laps later for the same

thing. Schrader went to pit road on lap 312 for right sides, which gave the lead to Morgan, who immediately dove for the pits for fuel only. Darrell Waltrip was the leader, but he had to come in for fuel on lap 318.

Morgan became the new leader, but Jarrett was on his heels. With nine laps remaining, Jarrett looked poised to pass the Citgo Ford. But it wasn't over. Ricky Rudd and Jeff Gordon got into it, and the ensuing yellow put the leaders in single file for the restart with three to go. Earnhardt and Terry Labonte had jumped on pit road for four fresh Goodyears, their only hope to win, but the rest remained in line on the track. The green flew, and Jarrett hammered inside Morgan to take the lead. Earnhardt, on fresh tires, looked like a Tomahawk missile on his way to the front, and Jarrett knew the black Chevrolet was on a mission.

But Michael Waltrip lost it, collected his brother on the backstretch and brought out the yellow with one lap to go. The race finished under yellow; Jarrett had manufactured his first victory since the 1993 Daytona 500. Shepherd was second, his best finish since the March Atlanta race, and Earnhardt finished third after rocketing up from the back of the field. Schrader rallied to fourth,

An early-race caution brings nearly the entire field to pit road for fuel, tires and chassis adjustments.

and Lake Speed came from 24th to fifth, his first top five since the spring Bristol race. Brett was sixth, Terry seventh and Derrike had a fine run to finish eighth in his new Ford. Darrell and Michael were credited with ninth and 10th, and Rusty was classified 37th.

Ward Burton had to wait out several delays during Pole Night qualifying (he was already the next to last in line to make an attempt!), but he took advantage of the cool night and blistered the track record to win the first Busch Pole of his young NASCAR Winston Cup career.

Fin. Pos.	Str. Pos.	Car #	Driver	Team	Fin. Pos.	Str. Pos.	Car #	Driver	Team
1	22	18	Dale Jarrett	Interstate Batteries Chevrolet	22	18	33	Harry Gant	Skoal Bandit Chevrolet
2	27	21	Morgan Shepherd	Citgo Ford	23	30	80	Joe Ruttman	Park Ohio Industries Ford
3	38	3	Dale Earnhardt	GM Goodwrench Chevrolet	24	3	43	John Andretti	STP Pontiac
4	11	25	Ken Schrader	Kodiak Chevrolet	25	31	8	Jeff Burton	Raybestos Ford
5	24	15	Lake Speed	Ford Quality Care Ford	26	42	29	Steve Grissom	DieHard Racing Chevrolet
6	8	26	Brett Bodine	Quaker State Ford	27	34	19	Loy Allen	Hooters Ford
7	9	5	Terry Labonte	Kellogg's Chevrolet	28	5	24	Jeff Gordon	DuPont Chevrolet
8	7	12	Derrike Cope	Straight Arrow Ford	29	16	10	Ricky Rudd	Tide Ford
9	35	17	Darrell Waltrip	Western Auto Chevrolet	30	41	42	Kyle Petty	Mello Yello Pontiac
10	2	30	Michael Waltrip	Pennzoil Pontiac	31	40	54	Robert Pressley	Manheim Auctions Chevrolet
11	4	41	Joe Nemechek	Meineke Chevrolet	32	6	7	Geoff Bodine	Exide Batteries Ford
12	19	1	Rick Mast	Skoal Classic Ford	33	28	11	Bill Elliott	Budweiser Ford
13	10	32	Dick Trickle	Sky Box International Chev	34	37	47	Billy Standridge	WCW/Dura-Lube Ford
14	21	28	Kenny Wallace	Texaco Havoline Ford	35	14	77	Greg Sacks	USAir Ford
15	36	44	Bobby Hillin	Buss Fuses Ford	36	23	4	Sterling Marlin	Kodak Film Chevrolet
16	25	27	Jimmy Spencer	McDonald's Ford	37	15	2	Rusty Wallace	Miller Genuine Draft Ford
17	13	90	Mike Wallace	Heilig-Meyers Ford	38	17	75	Todd Bodine	Factory Stores Ford
18	29	16	Ted Musgrave	The Family Channel Ford	39	12	6	Mark Martin	Valvoline Ford
19	26	40	Bobby Hamilton	Kendall Pontiac	40	39	20	Jimmy Hensley	Fina Lube Ford
20	32	98	Jeremy Mayfield	Fingerhut Ford	41	1	31	Ward Burton	Hardee's Chevrolet
21	33	23	Hut Stricklin	Smokin' Joe's Ford	42	20	22	Bobby Labonte	Maxwell House Pontiac

AC DELCO 500

NORTH CAROLINA
MOTOR SPEEDWAY

OCTOBER 23, 1994

The combination of Rusty Wallace's engine woes and Dale Earnhardt's meteoric drive through the field to claim third place at Charlotte resulted in a 321-point difference between the two as the teams unloaded at the newly repaved North Carolina Motor Speedway.

(Top) Mark Martin and Rusty Wallace fight for position on Rockingham's newly paved surface. Jeff Gordon is in hot pursuit. (Right) Dale Earnhardt wrapped up his seventh championship at Rockingham. It was the first time since 1987 that the Cup had been awarded before the season finale.

With just three races remaining on the schedule, Earnhardt was truly in the catbird seat at the one-miler in the Sand Hills. The Goodwrench Chevrolet team's stretch run was the stuff of champions — 10 top seven finishes in 11 races, including four thirds and three second places — and the team's work, combined with Dale's brilliant driving, had put the Kannapolis Comet in position to clinch his record-tying seventh NASCAR Winston Cup at Rockingham.

It would take a little doing — Dale needed to gain 50 points on Rusty to shut the Miller Ford driver out of the chase — but, for the first time since Earnhardt had claimed the crown in 1987 at Rockingham, it was possible that the Cup could be presented before season's end.

Wallace knew it was all but over. All the Missouri native could do was win, lead the most laps and hope Earnhardt had problems. Despite eight victories, Wallace knew his chances for a second title had all but vanished.

Testing on the new surface indicated that the old track record, set by Geoff Bodine (151.716 mph) in February, would fall. But no one expected the old mark to suffer a wholesale clobbering.

When qualifying finally was held (it was rained out the first day), 43 drivers brutalized the old mark in the first

1994
Winston Cup Champion
Dale Earnhardt

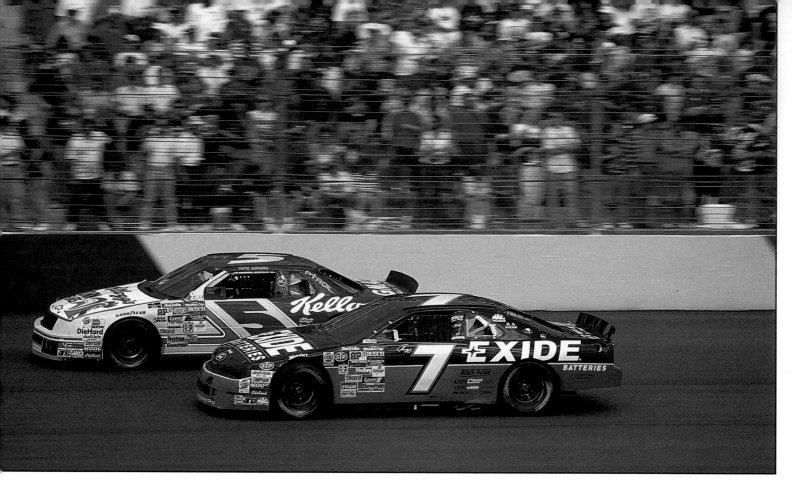

Geoff Bodine (7) and Terry Labonte jousted for the lead early in the race. Labonte won this battle by default when Geoff's motor blew – the latest in a series of such problems for the Exide team in 1994.

round. Ricky Rudd and his Tide Ford claimed the first pole of the season for the rookie team; Rudd's speed was almost six miles per hour faster than Bodine's old mark. For Rudd, it was a welcome payday. The pole qualified him for next February's Busch Clash, in which the last-place car earns $12,500.

With only two events remaining in the season, Ricky's pole eliminated the possibility that anyone could beat Geoff Bodine's record of five poles, allowing Bodine to clinch the year-end Busch Pole Award. Bodine's closest challenger had been Ernie Irvan (also with five), but that challenge had been resolved according to the first tie-breaker (five outside front-row spots to Ernie's one). Geoff qualified third for the AC Delco event, with Terry Labonte's Chevrolet sandwiched between the two fast Fords.

Derrike Cope continued to impress with his qualifying laps, earning the fourth-fastest position. Brett Bodine and Morgan

Shepherd were fifth and sixth, ahead of Ward Burton and Rick Mast. Harry Gant, in his final appearance in his home state, qualified ninth, ahead of Mark Martin. Rusty was 14th and Dale 20th following the first-session times.

Dick Trickle, who crashed during the first round, led the second-round qualifiers. Lake Speed and Bobby Hamilton were forced to take provisionals to get into the field. Hamilton wrecked a pair of Kendall Pontiacs

(left to right) Michael Waltrip, Dale Jarrett and Sterling Marlin were justifiably concerned before the start of the AC Delco 500. They had qualified 33rd, 27th and 37th, respectively, and would have to pit along the backstretch.

before the race started. Brad Noffsinger, Brad Teague and Norm Benning missed making the field.

Sunday morning, the NASCAR garage was hit by a bombshell: It was announced that Buddy Parrott, who had signed a two-year extension of his contract with Penske Racing just weeks ago, would leave the Miller team at the end of the current season. All indications were that Parrott would become the general manager of the Diamond Ridge team and work with Steve Grissom beginning in 1995.

The Penske slot became as huge an opportunity for a crew chief as the Yates Racing "28" car's seat was for a driver. At least five top crew chiefs applied on the spot to Rusty and fellow car owners Don Miller and Roger Penske.

Lining up the field for the start of the AC Delco 500 marked a historic occasion. Track officials had announced that next year's fall classic would be 400 miles; it would be the first time since the track's initial event in 1965 that competitors would race less than 500 miles.

From the start, the race had a familiar look. Geoff Bodine blasted to the point and then waltzed away from the field. Only Rick Mast was able to run with the black and blue Exide Ford.

Side by side Kennys. Wallace (28) and Schrader test the grooves in turn one as the field thunders by a capacity crowd at "The Rock."

Mast finally moved past Bodine on lap 61 but wrecked with Greg Sacks 25 laps later. Sacks was out, but Mast's crew kept the black and white Skoal Ford on the lead lap with superb work on pit road. Bodine faded from contention when his motor went sour, and he finally retired with engine failure.

Labonte, Gordon and Kenny Schrader then demonstrated the power of the Hendrick Motorsports effort, leading for 209 of the next 211 laps. Earnhardt fought his way through the field and took the lead from Schrader on lap 173, but he fell back immediately after gaining the five bonus points. Soon afterwards, Kenny's hopes for a

the race, the NASCAR Winston Cup would await him in victory lane.

Quick pit work put Earnhardt in the lead after a wreck which involved Mark Martin, Dave Marcis and Hut Stricklin. For the final third of the race, Earnhardt was in control. His only challengers were Mast, who had the Skoal Ford working well despite the damage, and Morgan Shepherd, who was driving his favorite Citgo Ford.

In the end, Mast produced the best challenge, but the Ford driver ran out of time in the waning laps. Rick, searching for his first career NASCAR Winston Cup win, closed on Earnhardt but didn't have enough to beat the black Chevrolet to the line. Behind Mast came Shepherd and Rudd, who rallied for a fourth-place finish. Terry Labonte and Bill Elliott took fifth and sixth, ahead of Martin and Trickle. Ward Burton and Speed claimed the final top 10 positions.

For the first time since the May Talladega race, the Goodwrench Chevrolet entered victory lane; the visit was well worth the wait. Not only did Earnhardt score the

win were dashed by a broken drive shaft. Gordon, whose "Rainbow Warriors" had set a new world record in winning the Unocal Pit Crew championship that Saturday afternoon, fell away with engine problems.

Wallace, who had won the last three Rockingham races, saw his chance for a title disintegrate when his Ford's engine disappeared in a plume of smoke on lap 303. He headed for the garage. If Dale could run until the end of

A disappointed Rusty Wallace conceded the championship to Earnhardt after his engine gave out for the second time in as many races.

first triumph in the fall Rockingham race of his career, but he was able to celebrate twice. After posing with the Rockingham trophy, it was time for The Big One.

Waiting for him was the seventh NASCAR Winston Cup of his career. For the third time, he had won titles back to back – all had occurred since he and car owner Richard Childress won their first title together in 1986. What had seemed impossible a decade ago had become reality: A driver had tied Richard Petty's career total of seven NASCAR Winston Cup championships.

Sterling Marlin's Kodak Chevrolet reveals the wear and tear of a long day at Rockingham. Despite the damage, Marlin climbed from his 37th-starting position to finish 14th. His running mate, Rick Carelli, finished in 22nd place.

Fin. Pos.	Str. Pos.	Car #	Driver	Team	Fin. Pos.	Str. Pos.	Car #	Driver	Team
1	20	3	Dale Earnhardt	GM Goodwrench Chevrolet	22	40	61	Rick Carelli	Total Petroleum Chevrolet
2	8	1	Rick Mast	Skoal Classic Ford	23	22	17	Darrell Waltrip	Western Auto Chevrolet
3	6	21	Morgan Shepherd	Citgo Ford	24	35	14	Randy McDonald	NTN Bearings Chevrolet
4	1	10	Ricky Rudd	Tide Ford	25	36	43	John Andretti	STP Pontiac
5	2	5	Terry Labonte	Kellogg's Corn Flakes Chevrolet	26	33	30	Michael Waltrip	Pennzoil Pontiac
6	18	11	Bill Elliott	Budweiser Ford	27	34	23	Hut Stricklin	Smokin' Joe's Ford
7	10	6	Mark Martin	Valvoline Ford	28	19	22	Bobby Labonte	Maxwell House Coffee Pontiac
8	21	32	Dick Trickle	SkyBox International Chevrolet	29	15	24	Jeff Gordon	DuPont Chevrolet
9	7	31	Ward Burton	Hardee's Chevrolet	30	16	29	Steve Grissom	DieHard Chevrolet
10	41	15	Lake Speed	Quality Care Ford	31	9	33	Harry Gant	Skoal Bandit Chevrolet
11	30	8	Jeff Burton	Raybestos Brakes Ford	32	24	25	Ken Schrader	Kodiak Chevrolet
12	27	18	Dale Jarrett	Interstate Batteries Chevrolet	33	42	40	Bobby Hamilton	Kendall Pontiac
13	26	16	Ted Musgrave	The Family Channel Ford	34	12	71	Dave Marcis	Terramite Chevrolet
14	37	4	Sterling Marlin	Kodak Film Chevrolet	35	14	2	Rusty Wallace	Miller Genuine Draft Ford
15	23	28	Kenny Wallace	Texaco Havoline Ford	36	29	42	Kyle Petty	Mello Yello Pontiac
16	31	90	Mike Wallace	Heilig-Meyers Ford	37	4	12	Derrike Cope	Straight Arrow Ford
17	13	41	Joe Nemechek	Meineke Mufflers Chevrolet	38	32	27	Jimmy Spencer	McDonald's Ford
18	5	26	Brett Bodine	Quaker State Ford	39	11	77	Greg Sacks	USAir Ford
19	39	98	Jeremy Mayfield	Fingerhut Ford	40	3	7	Geoff Bodine	Exide Batteries Ford
20	38	55	Butch Miller	RaDiUs Motorsports Ford	41	25	47	Billy Standridge	WCW/Dura-Lube Ford
21	28	75	Todd Bodine	Factory Stores of America Ford	42	17	19	Loy Allen	Hooters Ford

SLICK 50 500

PHOENIX INTERNATIONAL
RACEWAY

OCTOBER 30, 1994

Dale Earnhardt reveled in victory lane at Rockingham, enjoying the fruits of his successful quest for the 1994 NASCAR Winston Cup Championship. Dale hugged the trophy; then he hugged his wife, Teresa, and car owner Richard Childress. Then he surreptitiously sneaked a peek at his watch. The celebration continued, and Dale and his entourage headed for the press box for an interview session. He sneaked another peek.

(Top) Terry Labonte took the lead on lap 208 and led all but two of the final 105 laps on his way to victory lane. (Right) Fans packed the grandstands and spilled onto the hills in search of the perfect vantage point. On the track, drivers dealt with similar conditions as they tried to maneuver in extremely close quarters.

The sooner it all was over, the sooner he could jump on his plane, head for a shower in Statesville, NC, and fire up the Lear for the trip to New Mexico. The seven-time champion and Richard Childress, his friend, car owner and compatriot, were headed for the mountains for a long-scheduled elk hunting trip.

Little did either know that Childress would escape serious injury in what Dale and Richard later called "a hell of a horse-wreck!"

The trip from the hunting camp into the mountains was made on horseback. At one point, the climb up the mountain was so steep that the riders were forced to dismount and lead their horses up the crumbling, rock-strewn path. Childress was leading his horse up the trail, following Earnhardt and his horse, when Dale's mount slipped and began to slide off the rock. Dale tried to hold his horse but was forced to let go of the reins. As Dale released the reins, Childress dove to the side, out of the way. Horse and car owner fell about 50 feet down the side of the

Terry Labonte sets the pace at Buddy Jobe's beautiful one-mile oval.

mountain, and both landed in some pine trees. Richard was scratched and bloodied in the accident, but luckily, neither car owner nor horse suffered serious injury.

Later in the trip, both Earnhardt and Childress got their elk: Dale's was a 500-yard, single-shot kill.

By the time the two arrived in Phoenix for the Slick 50 500 at Buddy Jobe's modified desert oval, the two friends could joke about the "horse-wreck," but both quietly acknowledged that Richard was a lucky fellow to have avoided serious injury.

While Dale was telling his hunting trip tales, car owners Felix Sabates and Bud Moore were accepting congratulations from their peers in the garage area.

Sabates and driver Kyle Petty had announced Coors' sponsorship for the 1995 season; the SABCO Pontiac would carry the colors of Coors. Moore, who had been searching for a driver for the Quality Care Thunderbirds for '95 since Lake Speed had announced at Watkins Glen that he would not be back behind the wheel of the tri-tone blue Fords, had found the driver he wanted. Moore and the legendary Dick Trickle had signed a two-year contract; Trickle had agreed to leave the Active Trucking Chevrolets at the end of the '94 season.

The Slick 50 event was a combination NASCAR Winston Cup/Winston West race. With 54 cars on hand, it was obvious that nearly a dozen machines and drivers

would be forced to head home after the final qualifying session on Saturday. By the time Friday's session had been completed, Sterling Marlin had snapped a two-year drought and claimed the eighth pole of his career.

Rusty Wallace's championship chase had ended with engine failures at Charlotte and Rockingham, but the Miller Ford driver had now set his sights on winning at Phoenix and Atlanta; he wanted to equal his mark of 10 victories in 1993. But even if he was successful, it would be little consolation for the Missouri native. His poor luck at Daytona and Talladega had, once again, come back to haunt him in the point race.

Rusty did, however, claim the outside of the front row next to Marlin's picture-perfect Kodak Chevrolet. Bill Elliott and Ricky Rudd comprised the second row, and Dale Jarrett and Mark Martin were right behind. Kenny Schrader and Earnhardt were seventh and eighth. Brett Bodine and Speed occupied the fifth row.

It was evident that Goodyear had brought the right tire to Phoenix: Ward Burton was the highest Hoosier qualifier in 27th place! Hoosier-shod drivers such as the Burtons, Greg Sacks and Geoff Bodine wore markedly long faces. Jeremy Mayfield and Loy Allen claimed the provisionals, and Mike Chase, the NASCAR Winston West point leader, grabbed the final provisional spot of the 43-car field. Among those who went home were: Jeff Purvis, Brad Noffsinger, Scott Gaylord, Doug George, Jeff Davis, Joe Heath, Richard Woodland, John Krebs, St. James Davis, Lance Wade and Wayne Jacks.

Someone watching the Kellogg's corner of the garage area should have noticed the confidence oozing from the crew of the yellow and red Lumina. Terry Labonte, who had won at Richmond and North Wilkesboro earlier this season, had his flat-track special for Phoenix and was about to spring another surprise.

The first half of the Slick 50 500 belonged to Ricky

Before the race, Dick Trickle (32) announced his deal to drive Bud Moore's Fords in '95. Here, he dices with rookie contenders Steve Grissom (29) and Jeff Burton.

his Hendrick Motorsports mates. During the second half of the season, Terry had consistently been one of the best in the field. The Phoenix win was the third of the season for the cool Texan; it was the first season of his NASCAR Winston Cup career in which he had won more than two races.

Jeff Gordon, Ted Musgrave and Kyle Petty claimed the next three positions ahead of Rudd, Geoff Bodine and Dale Jarrett. Darrell Waltrip grabbed the final top 10 position. Rusty fought a good fight all day but couldn't find the handle on his Miller Ford. After finishing two laps behind in 17th place, he said he would add Phoenix to his test schedule for the coming season.

Where was Earnhardt? On his way back home. The newly crowned champion, who had been testing some "experimental" work on the engine in his Goodwrench Chevrolet, had found himself the victim of a cracked cylinder head. His race ended early at not quite one-third distance. Unfortunately for Wallace, the Goodwrench team's mechanical problems were too little, too late, with regard to returning the Penske driver to the point chase. Earnhardt was classified 40th, but it didn't matter. The

Rudd, but after a 30-minute red flag to repair wall damage, Rudd finally faded a little. Following the fourth and final caution flag, the race belonged to Mark Martin and Labonte. For the longest time, it appeared that Mark would finally win his second race of the year, but with 120 laps to go, Terry took the Lumina to the point and refused to yield. During the remainder of the race, he lost that position only during green-flag stops. As the race drew to its conclusion, Labonte merely kept upping the pressure; he pulled away to an easy three-second victory over the Valvoline Ford. Marlin fought his way to third place, the final car on the lead lap.

It was a stirring victory for Labonte and

Sterling Marlin piloted the Kodak Chevrolet to the pole with a record-setting lap of 129.833 mph.

NASCAR Winston Cup had already been awarded.

As the teams left the Valley of the Sun, Wallace looked at the points and realized he had another problem. Wallace's last three finishes, combined with those of Mark Martin, had pulled Mark to within 75 points in the battle for second place in the standings. Wallace was not alone – Kenny Schrader also studied the points only to discover that Ricky had pulled to within a single point in their battle for fourth in the standings.

Now, it all depended on Atlanta.

Upon his arrival in Phoenix, Bobby Hamilton (40) occupied the 25th slot in the point standings. He led Joe Nemechek (41) by a mere 37 points and Derrike Cope by 140.

Fin. Pos.	Str. Pos.	Car #	Driver	Team	Fin. Pos.	Str. Pos.	Car #	Driver	Team
1	19	5	Terry Labonte	Kellogg's Corn Flakes Chevrolet	23	24	33	Harry Gant	Skoal Bandit Chevrolet
2	6	6	Mark Martin	Valvoline Ford	24	31	23	Hut Stricklin	Smokin' Joe's Ford
3	1	4	Sterling Marlin	Kodak Film Chevrolet	25	16	41	Joe Nemechek	Meineke Mufflers Chevrolet
4	14	24	Jeff Gordon	DuPont Chevrolet	26	30	77	Greg Sacks	USAir Ford
5	12	16	Ted Musgrave	The Family Channel Ford	27	36	8	Jeff Burton	Raybestos Brakes Ford
6	15	42	Kyle Petty	Mello Yello Pontiac	28	26	90	Mike Wallace	Heilig-Meyers Ford
7	4	10	Ricky Rudd	Tide Ford	29	40	06	P.J. Jones	Ultra Racing Wheels Ford
8	37	7	Geoff Bodine	Exide Batteries Ford	30	22	12	Derrike Cope	Straight Arrow Ford
9	5	18	Dale Jarrett	Interstate Batteries Chevrolet	31	43	50	Mike Chase	Star Race Computers Chevrolet
10	18	17	Darrell Waltrip	Western Auto Chevrolet	32	23	75	Todd Bodine	Factory Stores of America Ford
11	29	40	Bobby Hamilton	Kendall Pontiac	33	32	61	Rick Carelli	Total Petroleum Chevrolet
12	13	21	Morgan Shepherd	Citgo Ford	34	38	76	Ron Hornaday, Jr.	Spears Motor Sports Chevrolet
13	9	26	Brett Bodine	Quaker State Ford	35	3	11	Bill Elliott	Budweiser Ford
14	10	15	Lake Speed	Quality Care Ford	36	25	30	Michael Waltrip	Pennzoil Pontiac
15	7	25	Ken Schrader	Kodiak Chevrolet	37	39	39	Rich Bickle	Pedigree Chevrolet
16	28	22	Bobby Labonte	Maxwell House Coffee Pontiac	38	20	27	Jimmy Spencer	McDonald's Ford
17	2	2	Rusty Wallace	Miller Genuine Draft Ford	39	35	32	Dick Trickle	Manheim Auctions Chevrolet
18	11	28	Kenny Wallace	Texaco Havoline Ford	40	8	3	Dale Earnhardt	GM Goodwrench Chevrolet
19	34	71	Dave Marcis	Prodigy Chevrolet	41	42	19	Loy Allen	Hooters Ford
20	41	98	Jeremy Mayfield	Fingerhut Ford	42	21	1	Rick Mast	Skoal Classic Ford
21	27	31	Ward Burton	Hardee's Chevrolet	43	17	43	John Andretti	STP Pontiac
22	33	29	Steve Grissom	Diamond Ridge Chevrolet					

HOOTERS 500

ATLANTA MOTOR
SPEEDWAY

NOVEMBER 13, 1994

The 500-mile contest at general manager Ed Clark's 1.5-mile Atlanta Motor Speedway was, for some drivers, the deciding event with regard to positions in the final point standings. For at least 10 driver and team combinations, the Hooters 500 marked the end of their associations.

And for one driver, it signaled the end of a career which began in 1964 with a Hobby Class car at Hickory, NC. The 1994 season was "The Bandit's Last Ride," and the day of Harry Gant's final NASCAR Winston Cup race finally had arrived.

Atlanta seemed the perfect place for Gant to end his career. At this same track, Harry nearly won the spring '81 race while driving a yellow and white Buick for Jack Beebe.

On that day in 1981, in a hospitality suite overlooking the track, Burt Reynolds and Hollywood director and stuntman Hal Needham, co-owners of Mach One Racing, viewed the race with interest. After watching Gant lead — seemingly at will — before losing to Cale Yarborough in the closing laps, Reynolds and Needham decided that the Taylorsville, NC, driver should join their Skoal Bandit team. At the time, Stan Barrett was the team's driver, but Gant's stirring performance had convinced both Reynolds and Needham that Harry needed to be a part of their team, even

(Top) In honor of Harry Gant's last Winston Cup race, Leo Jackson's team brought a surprise to Atlanta: The Lumina had been decorated with the same paint scheme originally used nearly fourteen years prior when Harry made his first ride for Skoal. (Right) A triumphant Mark Martin celebrated the conclusion of the 1994 season in style: He captured first place in the Hooters 500, his second victory of the year.

The "33" car bore the original, 1981 Skoal Bandit paint scheme, right down to the masked Bandit on the front hood and "Burt & Hal's" on the "B" pillar. The sight seemed to erase the 13 years that had passed since Gant became a "Bandit." The car beneath the paint wasn't a Pontiac, but the paint laid just as well on the sides of the Lumina as it had the Grand Prix some 14 years ago.

Many 1995 driver questions had been answered in the two weeks since Phoenix. Busch Grand National Series runner-up Ricky Craven had been named to drive the Larry Hedrick car, and Kodiak had moved to Hedrick as well to act as the sponsor. Dale Jarrett had been nominated to drive the Robert Yates Racing Fords for '95. Bobby Labonte had signed with Joe Gibbs as Jarrett's replacement after Bill Davis released Labonte from his contract. Meineke Mufflers announced at Atlanta that it would sponsor Gary Bechtel's Diamond Ridge team, for which Steve Grissom is the driver.

Atlanta had been re-paved since the March race, and testing had demonstrated that the track would be much faster than in the past. During Friday's first round of qualifying, the surprise pole-winner clocked in at nearly six miles per hour faster than the old record!

Greg Sacks had blistered the old mark, putting a lap of nearly 186 miles per hour on the board. Kenny Wallace tried his best with his Texaco Ford and Goodyear Eagles but came up just a tad short. Sacks, in the Hoosier-shod USAir Ford, had claimed his first pole of the season. Derrike Cope, driving the fast Ford fielded by Bobby Allison's team at Charlotte, plunked down the third-fastest lap and claimed the inside of the second row. Hoosier-runner Geoff Bodine started alongside Cope. Mark Martin and Jeff Gordon made up the third row, and rookie Joe Nemechek and a flu-ridden Ricky Rudd were

if it meant running two cars.

Within a matter of days, Gant was a Skoal Bandit; it was the beginning of an association that would last until the final race of the 1994 season. Hal and Burt dissolved their team at the end of the '88 season, but both were on hand to help celebrate Harry's final race at Atlanta. Burt was named the Grand Marshal for the race, and the return of Needham to the garage area was a welcome sight.

Harry and the Leo Jackson team, with the NFL's "throwback" uniforms in mind (the NFL had re-introduced original team uniforms in celebration of their 75th season), had concocted a treat for the fans, as well as Burt and Hal. Everyone in the garage area grinned with delight as the Lumina rolled off the Skoal transporter.

seventh- and eighth-fastest. Rounding out the top 10 were John Andretti and Terry Labonte. One of the surprises of the day was the starting position of ARCA rookie Gary Bradberry, who claimed the 12th-fastest lap with Jimmy Means' NAPA Ford.

Rusty Wallace was 18th. Winston Cup champion Dale Earnhardt was disgusted with himself — he did not make the field during the first day of qualifying. At the com-

It was clear from the start that tires would dictate the outcome of the final Hooters 500 (the event will change to the NAPA 500 next season). Neither brand of tires lasted a full fuel stop, so green flag stops were the order of the day. Some teams managed 20 laps on a set of tires, others economized to between 40 and 50 depending on the way the chassis were dialed in. Sacks and Geoff Bodine were the early rabbits, but Sacks cut a tire and

Even though the championship battle had been decided three weeks earlier, the Hooters 500 record crowd enjoyed a spectacular fall afternoon and witnessed the 1994 season draw to a close.

pletion of second-round qualifying, Kyle Petty and teammate Bobby Hamilton were forced to take provisionals to make the field, and Bill Elliott had to use a former champion's provisional. Those missing the race were: Tim Fedewa, Jeremy Mayfield, newcomer Gary Wright, Billy Standridge, Dick Trickle, Rich Bickle, Dave Marcis, Joe Ruttman, Bill Venturini, Brad Teague, Rick Carelli, Bob Brevak and Brian Bonner.

crunched the concrete. As a result, Sacks' right-front brake caliper came loose and ricocheted off the wall. Rusty Wallace, close behind Sacks, rolled over the piece, and it ping-ponged underneath his Miller Ford. Wallace's oil cooler and track bar were knocked off, and although he streaked to the garage for repairs, he was 62 laps behind by the time they were completed.

Two other accidents claimed Allen and his Hooters

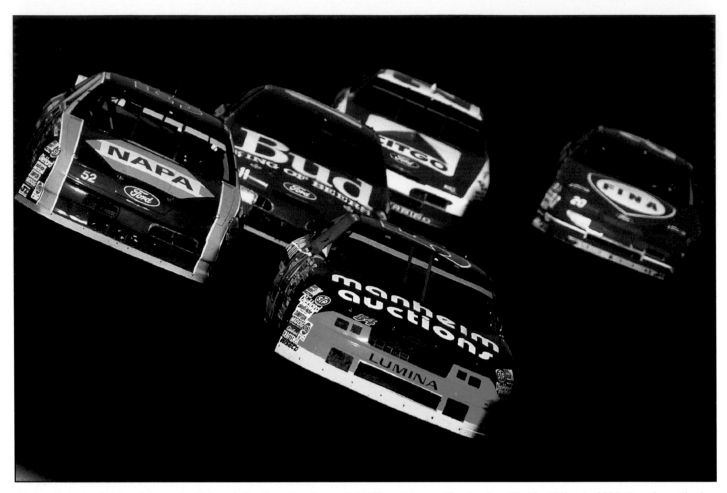

Robert Pressley leads a tight pack which includes Gary Bradberry, Bill Elliott, Morgan Shepherd and Bobby Hillin. In 1995, Pressley will take over the "33" car for retiring Harry Gant; Bill Elliott will trade Bud's red for McDonald's red; and NAPA will sponsor the final race of the season at Atlanta.

Ford (both Allen & Hooters will move to Junior Johnson's stable in 1995 and carry the number "27") and Geoff Bodine, who had recently returned to the track following repairs to a broken right-front shock absorber.

In the end, it came down to a battle between Martin, who ran conservatively through the first half of the race, and Earnhardt, who rallied from a lost lap after a green-flag stop. But when it was time to go, Mark put the Valvoline Ford into the wind, and the Goodwrench Chevrolet driver had nothing for him. Todd Bodine, after leading much of the final third of the race, came home a hugely satisfying third. Lake Speed, who led at regular intervals, was a fine fourth in his final drive in Bud Moore's Quality Care Ford. Mike Wallace, the Saturday ARCA race winner, diced superbly at the front throughout the day in Junie Donlavey's Heilig-Meyers Ford.

Morgan Shepherd recorded another solid run with the Wood Brothers' Ford and finished sixth, the final car on the lead lap. Cope, who ran in the top eight all day, faded after his final pit stop but took seventh, a lap down. Two laps back were Terry Labonte, Dale Jarrett and Michael Waltrip.

The combination of Mark's second victory of the year

and Rusty's troubles eased Martin into second place in the final point standings and dropped Wallace to third. Kenny Schrader finished 11th but managed to protect his lead over Rudd for fourth place in the standings. Shepherd was sixth in points ahead of Terry Labonte, Jeff Gordon, Darrell Waltrip and Bill Elliott. Lake finished 11th, and Michael Waltrip climbed two positions to 12th. The Monday following the race, Jeff Burton was named the MAXX Rookie of the Year after a year-long battle which included not only his brother, Ward, but top contenders Grissom, Andretti, Nemechek and Mike Wallace.

Gant's final season did not end the way he wished. He won two NASCAR Busch Series races and poles in both the Busch and Winston Cup Series, but failed to win in Cup competition. Despite the "throwback" paint scheme and positions as high as eighth in the race, the Skoal Lumina burned a piston: Harry was out of the race after 259 laps. He was classified 33rd in his final Winston Cup race.

The long season had come to a close. Dale Earnhardt had possessed the consistency needed to win championships. Rusty had led the circuit in victories, and Geoff

Jack Roush and crew chief Steve Hmiel are the "picture" of concentration as they coach their driver to victory in the 1994 Winston Cup season finale.

Bodine in Busch Poles. Not counting the year-end bonuses, Jeff Gordon had led in money won. A total of 12 drivers had visited victory lane, and the circuit had made a historic appearance at Indianapolis. In a couple of weeks, Earnhardt would be toasted at the annual banquet in New York and awarded his seventh Winston Cup.

It was hard to believe, but in just a matter of weeks, the tour would reassemble at Daytona, and a new battle for supremacy would begin.

Fin. Pos.	Str. Pos.	Car #	Driver	Team	Fin. Pos.	Str. Pos.	Car #	Driver	Team
1	5	6	Mark Martin	Valvoline Ford	23	7	41	Joe Nemechek	Meineke Mufflers Chevrolet
2	30	3	Dale Earnhardt	GM Goodwrench Chevrolet	24	42	40	Bobby Hamilton	Kendall Pontiac
3	36	75	Todd Bodine	Factory Stores of America Ford	25	2	28	Kenny Wallace	Texaco Havoline Ford
4	20	15	Lake Speed	Ford Quality Care Ford	26	29	29	Steve Grissom	Diamond Ridge Chevrolet
5	34	90	Mike Wallace	Heilig-Meyers Ford	27	24	1	Rick Mast	Skoal Classic Ford
6	33	21	Morgan Shepherd	Citgo Ford	28	21	16	Ted Musgrave	The Family Channel Ford
7	3	12	Derrike Cope	Straight Arrow Ford	29	40	67	Ken Bouchard	Cunningham Racing Ford
8	10	5	Terry Labonte	Kellogg's Corn Flakes Chevrolet	30	12	52	Gary Bradberry	NAPA Auto Parts Ford
9	23	18	Dale Jarrett	Interstate Batteries Chevrolet	31	19	8	Jeff Burton	Raybestos Brakes Ford
10	27	30	Michael Waltrip	Pennzoil Pontiac	32	18	2	Rusty Wallace	Miller Genuine Draft Ford
11	38	25	Ken Schrader	Kodiak Chevrolet	33	28	33	Harry Gant	Skoal Bandit Chevrolet
12	37	44	Jimmy Hensley	Buss Fuses Ford	34	4	7	Geoff Bodine	Exide Batteries Ford
13	9	43	John Andretti	STP Pontiac	35	35	54	Robert Pressley	Manheim Auctions Chevrolet
14	8	10	Ricky Rudd	Tide Ford	36	14	26	Brett Bodine	Quaker State Ford
15	6	24	Jeff Gordon	DuPont Chevrolet	37	11	22	Bobby Labonte	Maxwell House Coffee Pontiac
16	39	23	Hut Stricklin	Smokin' Joe's Ford	38	43	11	Bill Elliott	Budweiser Ford
17	22	78	Pancho Carter	Equipment Supply Ford	39	1	77	Greg Sacks	USAir Ford
18	31	97	Jeff Green	Ultra Wheel Ford	40	13	4	Sterling Marlin	Kodak Film Chevrolet
19	15	02	Randy LaJoie	Children's Miracle Network Ford	41	26	31	Ward Burton	Hardee's Chevrolet
20	25	27	Jimmy Spencer	McDonald's Ford	42	17	19	Loy Allen	Hooters Ford
21	16	17	Darrell Waltrip	Western Auto Chevrolet	43	32	20	Bobby Hillin	Fina Ford
22	41	42	Kyle Petty	Mello Yello Pontiac					

REFLECTIONS 1994

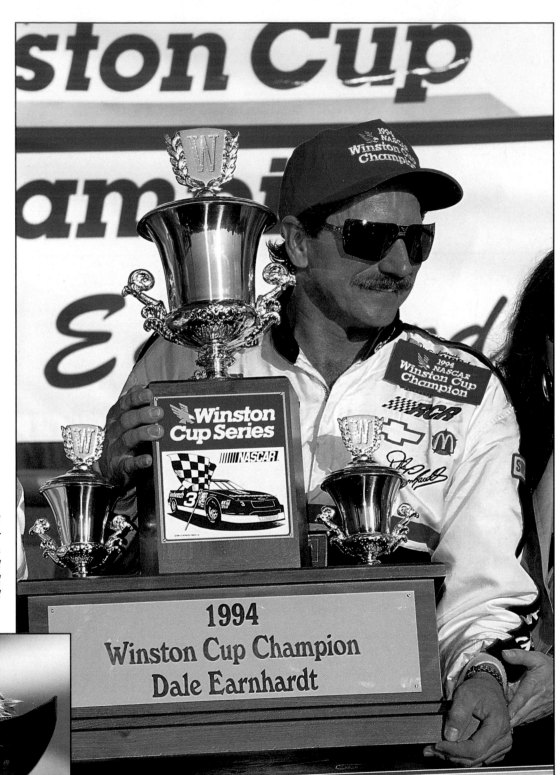

(Right) Seven and counting! *(Below)* Fifteen years after winning his seventh Winston Cup, Richard Petty watched Dale Earnhardt tie his record — one which many believed would never be matched.

Winston Cup Series

NASCAR

1994
Winston Cup Champion
Dale Earnhardt

(**Top**) *Pit crew performance and tire choice were among the big stories of 1994. Here, the Quality Care team performs their duties with alacrity.* (**Left**) *During the Coca-Cola 600, Mark Martin shows Jeff Gordon and Joe Nemechek "the groove." Gordon learned quickly and demonstrated his grasp of the concept by capturing his first career Winston Cup victory.* (**Bottom Left**) *Prior to his accident at Michigan, Ernie Irvan had been a leading contender for the Winston Cup championship. The grit, determination and courage upon which he has based his young racing career also explains, in large part, his remarkable recovery.* (**Bottom**) *Bill Elliott will return to Dawsonville for the 1995 season and trade his Budweiser sponsorship for McDonald's golden arches.*

(Top) The release of hundreds of thousands of gold and purple balloons signaled the start of the inaugural Brickyard 400. Jeff Gordon would later make history by winning the first-time event. (Left) Bobby Labonte shares a special moment with son Robert Tyler. (Bottom) The Winston Cup drivers battled Charlotte's treacherous turn four for the last time during the Coca-Cola 600. CMS was re-paved in the weeks following the race; Charlotte was one of four Winston Cup speedways to be resurfaced in 1994.

(Right) Harry Gant bid a fond farewell to fans across the country during "The Bandit's Last Ride." (Bottom) The Daytona 500 is an annual showcase for new cars, colors and sponsors.

(Top) Ken Schrader's strong showing in '94 was characterized by consistency, and his persistence paid dividends: He will proudly display the Budweiser logo in 1995. *(Right)* Fans have come to expect close racing at Talladega. Darrell Waltrip, Hut Stricklin, Joe Nemechek and Bobby Hamilton show everyone how it's done.

Kyle Petty hopes that "silver bullet" will describe not only his sponsorship but his racing style in 1995.

(Right) *The Valvoline crew escorts Mark Martin's Ford from famous Gasoline Alley. **(Overleaf)** NASCAR flagman Doyle Ford waves Rusty Wallace across the line as the winner of the Goody's 500 in Martinsville.*

Autographs

UMI Publications publishes the Official NASCAR Preview and Press Guide.
For subscription information, phone 704-374-0420.